SARAH PALIN

UNCUT

WORDS THAT CHANGED A NATION

SARAH PALIN

UNCUT

pac ps

Pacific Publishing Studio

Published in the United States by Pacific Publishing Studio.

www.PacPS.com

ISBN-13: 978-1456508326

ISBN-10: 1456508326

RNC Acceptance Speech

September 3, 2008

Mr. Chairman, delegates, and fellow citizens: I am honored to be considered for the nomination for vice president of the United States.

I accept the call to help our nominee for president to serve and defend America.

I accept the challenge of a tough fight in this election against confident opponents at a crucial hour for our country.

And I accept the privilege of serving with a man who has come through much harder missions ... and met far graver challenges and knows how tough fights are won—the next president of the United States, John S. McCain.

It was just a year ago when all the experts in Washington counted out our nominee because he refused to hedge his commitment to the security of the country he loves.

With their usual certitude, they told us that all was lost—there was no hope for this candidate who said that he would rather lose an election than see his country lose a war.

But the pollsters and pundits overlooked just one thing when they wrote him off.

They overlooked the caliber of the man himself—the determination, resolve, and sheer guts of Sen. John McCain. The voters knew better.

And maybe that's because they realize there is a time for politics and a time for leadership ... a time to campaign and a time to put our country first.

Our nominee for president is a true profile in courage, and people like that are hard to come by.

He's a man who wore the uniform of this country for 22 years and refused to break faith with those troops in Iraq who have now brought victory within sight.

And as the mother of one of those troops, that is exactly the kind of man I want as commander in chief. I'm just one of many moms who'll say an extra prayer each night for our sons and daughters going into harm's way.

Our son Track is 19. And one week from tomorrow—Sept. 11—he'll deploy to Iraq with the Army infantry in the service of his country.

My nephew Kasey also enlisted and serves on a carrier in the Persian Gulf.

My family is proud of both of them and of all the fine men and women serving the country in uniform. Track is the eldest of our five children.

In our family, it's two boys and three girls in between—my strong and kind-hearted daughters, Bristol, Willow and Piper.

And in April, my husband, Todd, and I welcomed our littlest one into the world, a perfectly beautiful baby boy named Trig. From the inside, no family ever seems typical.

That's how it is with us.

Our family has the same ups and downs as any other—the same challenges and the same joys.

Sometimes even the greatest joys bring challenge.

And children with special needs inspire a special love.

To the families of special-needs children all across this country, I have a message: For years, you sought to make America a more welcoming place for your sons and daughters.

I pledge to you that if we are elected, you will have a friend and advocate in the White House. Todd is a story all by himself.

He's a lifelong commercial fisherman ... a production operator in the oil fields of Alaska's North Slope ... a proud member of the United Steel Workers Union ... and world champion snow machine racer.

Throw in his Yup'ik Eskimo ancestry, and it all makes for quite a package.

We met in high school, and two decades and five children later he's still my guy. My mom and dad both worked at the elementary school in our small town.

And among the many things I owe them is one simple lesson: that this is America, and every woman can walk through every door of opportunity.

My parents are here tonight, and I am so proud to be the daughter of Chuck and Sally Heath. Long ago, a young farmer and haberdasher from Missouri followed an unlikely path to the vice presidency.

A writer observed: "We grow good people in our small towns, with honesty, sincerity, and dignity." I know just the kind of people that writer had in mind when he praised Harry Truman.

I grew up with those people.

They are the ones who do some of the hardest work in America who grow our food, run our factories and fight our wars.

They love their country, in good times and bad, and they're always proud of America. I had the privilege of living most of my life in a small town.

I was just your average hockey mom and signed up for the PTA because I wanted to make my kids' public education better.

When I ran for City Council, I didn't need focus groups and voter profiles because I knew those voters, and knew their families, too.

Before I became governor of the great state of Alaska, I was mayor of my hometown.

And since our opponents in this presidential election seem to look down on that experience, let me explain to them what the job involves.

I guess a small-town mayor is sort of like a "community organizer," except that you have actual responsibilities. I might add that in small towns, we don't quite know what to make of a candidate who lavishes praise on working people when they are listening, and then talks about how bitterly they cling to their religion and guns when those people aren't listening.

We tend to prefer candidates who don't talk about us one way in Scranton and another way in San Francisco.

As for my running mate, you can be certain that wherever he goes, and whoever is listening, John McCain is the same man. I'm not a member of the permanent political establishment. And I've learned quickly, these past few days, that if you're not a member in good standing of the Washington elite, then some in the media consider a candidate unqualified for that reason alone.

But here's a little news flash for all those reporters and commentators: I'm not going to Washington to seek their good opinion. I'm going to Washington to serve the people of this country. Americans expect us to go to Washington for the right reasons, and not just to mingle with the right people.

Politics isn't just a game of clashing parties and competing interests.

The right reason is to challenge the status quo, to serve the common good, and to leave this nation better than we found it.

No one expects us to agree on everything.

But we are expected to govern with integrity, good will, clear convictions, and ... a servant's heart.

I pledge to all Americans that I will carry myself in this spirit as vice president of the United States. This was the spirit that brought me to the governor's office, when I took on the old politics as usual in Juneau ... when I stood up to the special interests, the lobbyists, big oil companies, and the good-ol' boys network.

Sudden and relentless reform never sits well with entrenched interests and power brokers. That's why true reform is so hard to achieve.

But with the support of the citizens of Alaska, we shook things up.

And in short order we put the government of our state back on the side of the people.

I came to office promising major ethics reform, to end the culture of self-dealing. And today, that ethics reform is the law.

While I was at it, I got rid of a few things in the governor's office that I didn't believe our citizens should have to pay for.

That luxury jet was over the top. I put it on eBay.

I also drive myself to work.

And I thought we could muddle through without the governor's personal chef—although I've got to admit that sometimes my kids sure miss her. I came to office promising to control spending—by request if possible and by veto if necessary.

Sen. McCain also promises to use the power of veto in defense of the public interest—and as a chief executive, I can assure you it works.

Our state budget is under control.

We have a surplus.

And I have protected the taxpayers by vetoing wasteful spending: nearly half a billion dollars in vetoes.

I suspended the state fuel tax and championed reform to end the abuses of earmark spending by Congress.

I told the Congress "thanks, but no thanks," for that Bridge to Nowhere.

If our state wanted a bridge, we'd build it ourselves. When oil and gas prices went up dramatically, and filled up the state treasury, I sent a large share of that revenue back where it belonged—directly to the people of Alaska.

And despite fierce opposition from oil company lobbyists, who kind of liked things the way they were, we broke their monopoly on power and resources.

As governor, I insisted on competition and basic fairness to end their control of our state and return it to the people.

I fought to bring about the largest private-sector infrastructure project in North American history.

And when that deal was struck, we began a nearly 40 billion-dollar natural gas pipeline to help lead America to energy independence.

That pipeline, when the last section is laid and its valves are opened, will lead America one step farther away from dependence on dangerous foreign powers that do not have our interests at heart.

The stakes for our nation could not be higher.

When a hurricane strikes in the Gulf of Mexico, this country should not be so dependent on imported oil that we are forced to draw from our Strategic Petroleum Reserve.

And families cannot throw away more and more of their paychecks on gas and heating oil.

With Russia wanting to control a vital pipeline in the Caucasus, and to divide and intimidate our European allies by using energy as a weapon, we cannot leave ourselves at the mercy of foreign suppliers.

To confront the threat that Iran might seek to cut off nearly a fifth of world energy supplies ... or that terrorists might strike again at the Abqaiq facility in Saudi Arabia ... or that Venezuela might shut off its oil deliveries ... we Americans need to produce more of our own oil and gas.

And take it from a gal who knows the North Slope of Alaska: We've got lots of both.

Our opponents say, again and again, that drilling will not solve all of America's energy problems—as if we all didn't know that already.

But the fact that drilling won't solve every problem is no excuse to do nothing at all.

Starting in January, in a McCain-Palin administration, we're going to lay more pipelines ... build more nuclear plants ... create jobs with clean coal ... and move forward on solar, wind, geothermal and other alternative sources.

We need American energy resources, brought to you by American ingenuity, and produced by American workers. I've noticed a pattern with our opponent.

Maybe you have, too.

We've all heard his dramatic speeches before devoted followers.

And there is much to like and admire about our opponent.

But listening to him speak, it's easy to forget that this is a man who has authored two memoirs but not a single major law or reform—not even in the state Senate.

This is a man who can give an entire speech about the wars America is fighting and never use the word "victory" except when he's talking about his own campaign. But when the cloud of rhetoric has passed ... when the roar of the crowd fades away ... when the stadium lights go out, and those

Styrofoam Greek columns are hauled back to some studio lot—what exactly is our opponent's plan? What does he actually seek to accomplish, after he's done turning back the waters and healing the planet? The answer is to make government bigger ... take more of your money ... give you more orders from Washington ... and to reduce the strength of America in a dangerous world. America needs more energy ... our opponent is against producing it.

Victory in Iraq is finally in sight ... he wants to forfeit.

Terrorist states are seeking nuclear weapons without delay ... he wants to meet them without preconditions.

Al-Qaida terrorists still plot to inflict catastrophic harm on America ... he's worried that someone won't read them their rights? Government is too big ... he wants to grow it.

Congress spends too much ... he promises more.

Taxes are too high ... he wants to raise them. His tax increases are the fine print in his economic plan, and let me be specific.

The Democratic nominee for president supports plans to raise income taxes ... raise payroll taxes ... raise investment income taxes ... raise the death tax ... raise business taxes ... and increase the tax burden on the American people by hundreds of billions of dollars. My sister Heather and her husband have just built a service station that's now opened for business—like millions of others who run small businesses.

How are they going to be any better off if taxes go up? Or maybe you're trying to keep your job at a plant in Michigan or Ohio ... or create jobs with clean coal from Pennsylvania or West Virginia ... or keep a small farm in the family right here in Minnesota.

How are you going to be better off if our opponent adds a massive tax burden to the American economy? Here's how I look at the choice Americans face in this election.

In politics, there are some candidates who use change to promote their careers.

And then there are those, like John McCain, who use their careers to promote change.

They're the ones whose names appear on laws and landmark reforms, not just on buttons and banners, or on self-designed presidential seals.

Among politicians, there is the idealism of high-flown speechmaking, in which crowds are stirringly summoned to support great things.

And then there is the idealism of those leaders, like John McCain, who actually do great things. They're the ones who are good for more than talk ... the ones we have always been able to count on to serve and defend America. Sen. McCain's record of actual achievement and reform helps explain why so many special interests, lobbyists and comfortable committee chairmen in Congress have fought the prospect of a McCain presidency—from the primary election of 2000 to this very day.

Our nominee doesn't run with the Washington herd.

He's a man who's there to serve his country, and not just his party.

A leader who's not looking for a fight, but is not afraid of one either. Harry Reid, the majority leader of the current do-nothing Senate, not long ago summed up his feelings about our nominee.

He said, quote, "I can't stand John McCain." Ladies and gentlemen, perhaps no accolade we hear this week is better proof that we've chosen the right man. Clearly what the majority leader was driving at is that he can't stand up to John McCain. That is only one more reason to take the maverick of the Senate and put him in the White House. My fellow citizens, the American presidency is not supposed to be a journey of "personal discovery." This world of threats and dangers is not just a community, and it doesn't just need an organizer.

And though both Sen. Obama and Sen. Biden have been going on lately about how they are always, quote, "fighting for you," let us face the matter squarely.

There is only one man in this election who has ever really fought for you ... in places where winning means survival and defeat means death ... and that man is John McCain. In our day, politicians have readily shared much lesser tales of adversity than the nightmare world in which this man, and others equally brave, served and suffered for their country.

It's a long way from the fear and pain and squalor of a 6-by-4 cell in Hanoi to the Oval Office.

But if Sen. McCain is elected president, that is the journey he will have made.

It's the journey of an upright and honorable man—the kind of fellow whose name you will find on war memorials in small towns across this country, only he was among those who came home.

To the most powerful office on Earth, he would bring the compassion that comes from having once been powerless ... the wisdom that comes even to the captives, by the grace of God ... the special confidence of those who have seen evil, and seen how evil is overcome. A fellow prisoner of war, a man named Tom Moe of Lancaster, Ohio, recalls looking through a pinhole in his cell door as Lt. Cmdr. John McCain was led down the hallway, by the guards, day after day.

As the story is told, "When McCain shuffled back from torturous interrogations, he would turn toward Moe's door and flash a grin and thumbs up"—as if to say, "We're going to pull through this." My fellow Americans, that is the kind of man America needs to see us through these next four years.

For a season, a gifted speaker can inspire with his words.

For a lifetime, John McCain has inspired with his deeds.

If character is the measure in this election ... and hope the theme ... and change the goal we share, then I ask you to join our cause. Join our cause and help America elect a great man as the next president of the United States.

Thank you all, and may God bless America."

The Vice-Presidential Debate

October 2, 2008

GWEN IFILL: Good evening from Washington University in St. Louis, Missouri. I'm Gwen Ifill of "The NewsHour" and "Washington Week" on PBS. Welcome to the first and the only 2008 vice presidential debate between the Republican nominee, Governor Sarah Palin of Alaska, and the Democratic nominee, Joe Biden of Delaware.

The Commission on Presidential Debates is the sponsor of this event and the two remaining presidential debates. Tonight's discussion will cover a wide range of topics, including domestic and foreign policy matters.

It will be divided roughly into five-minute segments. Each candidate will have 90 seconds to respond to a direct question and then an additional two minutes for rebuttal and follow-up. The order has been determined by a coin toss.

The specific subjects and questions were chosen by me and have not been shared or cleared with anyone on the campaigns or on the commission. The audience here in the hall has promised to remain very polite, no cheers, applause, no untoward outbursts, except right at this minute now, as we welcome Governor Palin and Senator Biden.

PALIN: Nice to meet you.

BIDEN: It's a pleasure.

PALIN: Hey, can I call you Joe?

BIDEN: (OFF-MIKE)

PALIN: Thank you. Thank you, Gwen. Thank you. Thank you.

IFILL: Welcome to you both.

As we have determined by a coin toss, the first question will go to Senator Biden, with a 90-second follow-up from Governor Palin.

The House of Representatives this week passed a bill, a big bailout bill—or didn't pass it, I should say. The Senate decided to pass it, and the House is wrestling with it still tonight.

As America watches these things happen on Capitol Hill, Senator Biden, was this the worst of Washington or the best of Washington that we saw play out?

BIDEN: Let me begin by thanking you, Gwen, for hosting this.

And, Governor, it's a pleasure to meet you, and it's a pleasure to be with you.

I think it's neither the best or worst of Washington, but it's evidence of the fact that the economic policies of the last eight years have been the worst economic policies we've ever had. As a consequence, you've seen what's happened on Wall Street.

15

If you need any more proof positive of how bad the economic theories have been, this excessive deregulation, the failure to oversee what was going on, letting Wall Street run wild, I don't think you needed any more evidence than what you see now.

So the Congress has been put—Democrats and Republicans have been put in a very difficult spot. But Barack Obama laid out four basic criteria for any kind of rescue plan here.

He, first of all, said there has to be oversight. We're not going to write any check to anybody unless there's oversight for the—of the secretary of Treasury.

He secondly said you have to focus on homeowners and folks on Main Street.

Thirdly, he said that you have to treat the taxpayers like investors in this case.

And, lastly, what you have to do is make sure that CEOs don't benefit from this, because this could end up, in the long run, people making money off of this rescue plan.

And so, as a consequence of that, it brings us back to maybe the fundamental disagreement between Governor Palin and me and Senator McCain and Barack Obama, and that is that the—we're going to fundamentally change the focus of the economic policy.

We're going to focus on the middle class, because it's—when the middle class is growing, the economy grows and everybody does well, not just focus on the wealthy and corporate America.

IFILL: Thank you, Senator. Governor Palin?

PALIN: Thank you, Gwen. And I thank the commission, also. I appreciate this privilege of being able to be here and speak with Americans.

You know, I think a good barometer here, as we try to figure out has this been a good time or a bad time in America's economy, is go to a kid's soccer game on Saturday, and turn to any parent there on the sideline and ask them, "How are you feeling about the economy?"

And I'll bet you, you're going to hear some fear in that parent's voice, fear regarding the few investments that some of us have in the stock market. Did we just take a major hit with those investments?

Fear about, how are we going to afford to send our kids to college? A fear, as small-business owners, perhaps, how we're going to borrow any money to increase inventory or hire more people.

The barometer there, I think, is going to be resounding that our economy is hurting and the federal government has not provided the sound oversight that we need and that we deserve, and we need reform to that end.

Now, John McCain thankfully has been one representing reform. Two years ago, remember, it was John McCain who pushed so hard with the Fannie Mae and Freddie Mac reform measures. He sounded that warning bell.

People in the Senate with him, his colleagues, didn't want to listen to him and wouldn't go towards that reform that was needed then. I think that the alarm has been heard, though, and there will be that greater oversight, again thanks to John McCain's bipartisan efforts that he was so instrumental in bringing folks together over this past week, even suspending his own campaign to make sure he was putting excessive politics aside and putting the country first.

IFILL: You both would like to be vice president.

Senator Biden, how, as vice president, would you work to shrink this gap of polarization which has sprung up in Washington, which you both have spoken about here tonight?

BIDEN: Well, that's what I've done my whole career, Gwen, on very, very controversial issues, from dealing with violence against women, to putting 100,000 police officers on the street, to trying to get something done about the genocide in—that was going on in Bosnia.

And I—I have been able to reach across the aisle. I think it's fair to say that I have almost as many friends on the Republican side of the aisle as I do the Democratic side of the aisle.

But am I able to respond to—are we able to stay on the—on the topic?

IFILL: You may, if you like.

BIDEN: Yes, well, you know, until two weeks ago—it was two Mondays ago John McCain said at 9 o'clock in the morning that the fundamentals of the economy were strong. Two weeks before that, he said George—we've made great economic progress under George Bush's policies.

Nine o'clock, the economy was strong. Eleven o'clock that same day, two Mondays ago, John McCain said that we have an economic crisis.

That doesn't make John McCain a bad guy, but it does point out he's out of touch. Those folks on the sidelines knew that two months ago.

IFILL: Governor Palin, you may respond.

PALIN: John McCain, in referring to the fundamental of our economy being strong, he was talking to and he was talking about the American workforce. And the American workforce is the greatest in this world, with the ingenuity and the work ethic that is just entrenched in our workforce. That's a positive. That's encouragement. And that's what John McCain meant.

Now, what I've done as a governor and as a mayor is huge. I've had that track record of reform. And I've joined this team that is a team of mavericks with John McCain, also, with his track record of reform, where we're known for putting partisan politics aside to just get the job done.

Now, Barack Obama, of course, he's pretty much only voted along his party lines. In fact, 96 percent of his votes have been solely along party line, not having that proof for the American people to know that his commitment, too, is, you know, put the partisanship, put the special interests aside, and get down to getting business done for the people of America.

We're tired of the old politics as usual. And that's why, with all due respect, I do respect your years in the U.S. Senate, but I think Americans are craving something new and different and that new energy and that new commitment that's going to come with reform.

I think that's why we need to send the maverick from the Senate and put him in the White House, and I'm happy to join him there.

IFILL: Governor, Senator, neither of you really answered that last question about what you would do as vice president. I'm going to come back to that throughout the evening to try to see if we can look forward, as well.

Now, let's talk about—the next question is to talk about the subprime lending meltdown.

Who do you think was at fault? I start with you, Governor Palin. Was it the greedy lenders? Was it the risky home-buyers who shouldn't have been buying a home in the first place? And what should you be doing about it?

PALIN: Darn right it was the predator lenders, who tried to talk Americans into thinking that it was smart to buy a $300,000 house if we could only afford a $100,000 house. There was deception there, and there was greed and there is corruption on Wall Street. And we need to stop that.

Again, John McCain and I, that commitment that we have made, and we're going to follow through on that, getting rid of that corruption.

PALIN: One thing that Americans do at this time, also, though, is let's commit ourselves just every day American people, Joe Six Pack, hockey moms across the nation, I think we need to band together and say never again. Never will we be exploited and taken advantage of again by those who are managing our money and loaning us these dollars. We need to make sure that we demand from the federal government strict oversight of those entities in charge of our investments and our savings and we need also to not get ourselves in debt. Let's do what our parents told us before we probably even got that first credit card. Don't live outside of our means. We need to make sure that as individuals we're taking personal responsibility through all of this. It's not the American peoples fault that the economy is hurting like it is, but we have an opportunity to learn a heck of a lot of good lessons through this and say never again will we be taken advantage of.

IFILL: Senator?

BIDEN: Well Gwen, two years ago Barack Obama warned about the subprime mortgage crisis. John McCain said shortly after that in December he was surprised there was a subprime mortgage problem. John McCain while Barack Obama was warning about what we had to do was literally giving an interview to "The Wall Street Journal" saying that I'm always for cutting regulations. We let Wall Street run wild. John McCain and he's a good man, but John McCain thought the answer is that tried and true Republican response, deregulate, deregulate.

So what you had is you had overwhelming "deregulation." You had actually the belief that Wall Street could self-regulate itself. And while Barack Obama was talking about reinstating those regulations, John on 20 different occasions in the previous year and a half called for more deregulation. As a matter of fact, John recently wrote an article in a major magazine saying that he wants to do for the health care industry deregulate it and let the free market move like he did for the banking industry.

So deregulation was the promise. And guess what? Those people who say don't go into debt, they can barely pay to fill up their gas tank. I was recently at my local gas station and asked a guy named Joey Danco. I said Joey, how much did it cost to fill your tank? You know what his answer was? He said I don't know, Joe. I never have enough money to do it. The middle class needs relief, tax relief. They need it now. They need help now. The focus will change with Barack Obama.

IFILL: Governor, please if you want to respond to what he said about Senator McCain's comments about health care?

PALIN: I would like to respond about the tax increases. We can speak in agreement here that darn right we need tax relief for Americans so that jobs can be created here. Now, Barack Obama and Senator Biden also voted for the largest tax increases in U.S. history. Barack had 94 opportunities to side on the people's side and reduce taxes and 94 times he voted to increase taxes or not support a tax reduction, 94 times.

Now, that's not what we need to create jobs and really bolster and heat up our economy. We do need the private sector to be able to keep more of what we earn and produce. Government is going to have to learn to be more efficient and live with less if that's what it takes to reign in the government growth that we've seen today. But we do need tax relief and Barack Obama even supported increasing taxes as late as last year for those families making only $42,000 a year. That's a lot of middle income average American families to increase taxes on them. I think that is the way to kill jobs and to continue to harm our economy.

IFILL: Senator?

BIDEN: The charge is absolutely not true. Barack Obama did not vote to raise taxes. The vote she's referring to, John McCain voted the exact same way. It was a budget procedural vote. John McCain voted the same way. It did not raise taxes. Number two, using the standard that the governor uses, John McCain voted 477 times to raise taxes. It's a bogus standard it but if you notice, Gwen, the governor did not answer the question about deregulation, did not answer the question of defending John McCain about not going along with the deregulation, letting Wall Street run wild. He did support deregulation almost across the board. That's why we got into so much trouble.

IFILL: Would you like to have an opportunity to answer that before we move on?

PALIN: I'm still on the tax thing because I want to correct you on that again. And I want to let you know what I did as a mayor and as a governor. And I may not answer the questions the way that either the moderator or you want to hear, but I'm going to talk straight to the American people and let them know my track record also. As mayor, every year I was in office I did reduce taxes. I eliminated personal property taxes and eliminated small business inventory taxes and as governor we suspended our state fuel tax. We did all of those things knowing that that is how our economy would be heated up. Now, as for John McCain's adherence to rules and regulations and pushing for even harder and tougher regulations, that is another thing that he is known for though. Look at the tobacco industry. Look at campaign finance reform.

IFILL: OK, our time is up here. We've got to move to the next question. Senator Biden, we want to talk about taxes, let's talk about taxes. You proposed raising taxes on people who earn over $250,000 a year. The question for you is, why is that not class warfare and the same question for you, Governor Palin, is you have proposed a tax employer health benefits which some studies say would actually throw five million more people onto the roles of the uninsured. I want to know why that isn't taking things out on the poor, starting with you, Senator Biden.

BIDEN: Well Gwen, where I come from, it's called fairness, just simple fairness. The middle class is struggling. The middle class under John McCain's tax proposal, 100 million families, middle class families, households to be precise, they got not a single change, they got not a single break in taxes. No one making less than $250,000 under Barack Obama's plan will see one single penny of their tax raised whether it's their capital gains tax, their income tax, investment tax, any tax. And 95 percent of the people in the United States of America making less than $150,000 will get a tax break.

Now, that seems to me to be simple fairness. The economic engine of America is middle class. It's the people listening to this broadcast. When you do well, America does well. Even the wealthy do well. This is not punitive. John wants to add $300 million, billion in new tax cuts per year for corporate America and the very wealthy while giving virtually nothing to the middle class. We have a different value set. The middle class is the economic engine. It's fair. They deserve the tax breaks, not the super wealthy who are doing pretty well. They don't need any more tax breaks. And by the way, they'll pay no more than they did under Ronald Reagan.

IFILL: Governor?

PALIN: I do take issue with some of the principle there with that redistribution of wealth principle that seems to be espoused by you. But when you talk about Barack's plan to tax increase affecting only those making $250,000 a year or more, you're forgetting millions of small businesses that are going to fit into that category. So they're going to be the ones paying higher taxes thus resulting in fewer jobs being created and less productivity.

Now you said recently that higher taxes or asking for higher taxes or paying higher taxes is patriotic. In the middle class of America which is where Todd and I have been all of our lives, that's not patriotic. Patriotic is saying, government, you know, you're not always the solution. In fact, too often you're the problem so, government, lessen the tax burden and on our families and get out of the way and let the private sector and our families grow and thrive and prosper. An increased tax formula that Barack Obama is proposing in addition to nearly a trillion dollars in new spending that he's proposing is the backwards way of trying to grow our economy.

IFILL: Governor, are you interested in defending Senator McCain's health care plan?

PALIN: I am because he's got a good health care plan that is detailed. And I want to give you a couple details on that. He's proposing a $5,000 tax credit for families so that they can get out there and they can purchase their own health care coverage. That's a smart thing to do. That's budget neutral. That doesn't cost the government anything as opposed to Barack Obama's plan to mandate health care coverage and have universal government run program and unless you're pleased with the way the federal government has been running anything lately, I don't think that it's going to be real pleasing for Americans to consider health care being taken over by the feds. But a $5,000 health care credit through our income tax that's budget neutral. That's going to help. And he also wants to erase those artificial lines between states so that through competition, we can cross state lines and if there's a better plan offered somewhere else, we would be able to purchase that. So affordability and accessibility will be the keys there with that $5,000 tax credit also being offered.

IFILL: Thank you, governor. Senator?

BIDEN: Gwen, I don't know where to start. We don't call a redistribution in my neighborhood Scranton, Claymont, Wilmington, the places I grew up, to give the fair to say that not giving Exxon Mobil another $4 billion tax cut this year as John calls for and giving it to middle class people to be able to pay to get their kids to college, we don't call that redistribution. We call that fairness number one. Number two fact, 95 percent of the small businesses in America, their owners make less than $250,000 a year. They would not get one single solitary penny increase in taxes, those small businesses.

BIDEN: Now, with regard to the—to the health care plan, you know, it's with one hand you giveth, the other you take it. You know how Barack Obama—excuse me, do you know how John McCain pays for his $5,000 tax credit you're going to get, a family will get?

He taxes as income every one of you out there, every one of you listening who has a health care plan through your employer. That's how he raises $3.6 trillion, on your—taxing your health care benefit to give you a $5,000 plan, which his Web site points out will go straight to the insurance company.

And then you're going to have to replace a $12,000—that's the average cost of the plan you get through your employer—it costs $12,000. You're going to have to pay—replace a $12,000 plan, because 20 million of you are going to be dropped. Twenty million of you will be dropped.

So you're going to have to place—replace a $12,000 plan with a $5,000 check you just give to the insurance company. I call that the "Ultimate Bridge to Nowhere."

IFILL: Thank you, Senator.

Now... I want to get—try to get you both to answer a question that neither of your principals quite answered when my colleague, Jim Lehrer, asked it last week, starting with you, Senator Biden.

What promises—given the events of the week, the bailout plan, all of this, what promises have you and your campaigns made to the American people that you're not going to be able to keep?

BIDEN: Well, the one thing we might have to slow down is a commitment we made to double foreign assistance. We'll probably have to slow that down.

We also are going to make sure that we do not go forward with the tax cut proposals of the administration—of John McCain, the existing one for people making over $250,000, which is $130 billion this year alone.

We're not going to support the $300 billion tax cut that they have for corporate America and the very wealthy. We're not going to support another $4 billion tax cut for ExxonMobil.

And what we're not going to also hold up on, Gwen, is we cannot afford to hold up on providing for incentives for new jobs by an energy policy, creating new jobs.

We cannot slow up on education, because that's the engine that is going to give us the economic growth and competitiveness that we need.

And we are not going to slow up on the whole idea of providing for affordable health care for Americans, none of which, when we get to talk about health care, is as my—as the governor characterized—characterized.

The bottom line here is that we are going to, in fact, eliminate those wasteful spending that exist in the budget right now, a number of things I don't have time, because the light is blinking, that I won't be able to mention, but one of which is the $100 billion tax dodge that, in fact, allows people to take their post office box off- shore, avoid taxes.

I call that unpatriotic. I call that unpatriotic.

IFILL: Governor?

BIDEN: That's what I'm talking about.

IFILL: Governor?

PALIN: Well, the nice thing about running with John McCain is I can assure you he doesn't tell one thing to one group and then turns around and tells something else to another group, including his plans that will make this bailout plan, this rescue plan, even better.

I want to go back to the energy plan, though, because this is—this is an important one that Barack Obama, he voted for in '05.

Senator Biden, you would remember that, in that energy plan that Obama voted for, that's what gave those oil companies those big tax breaks. Your running mate voted for that.

You know what I had to do in the state of Alaska? I had to take on those oil companies and tell them, "No," you know, any of the greed there that has been kind of instrumental, I guess, in their mode of operation, that wasn't going to happen in my state.

And that's why Tillerson at Exxon and Mulva at ConocoPhillips, bless their hearts, they're doing what they need to do, as corporate CEOs, but they're not my biggest fans, because what I had to do up there in Alaska was to break up a monopoly up there and say, you know, the people are going to come first and we're going to make sure that we have value given to the people of Alaska with those resources.

And those huge tax breaks aren't coming to the big multinational corporations anymore, not when it adversely affects the people who live in a state and, in this case, in a country who should be benefiting at the same time. So it was Barack Obama who voted for that energy plan that gave those tax breaks to the oil companies that I then had to turn around, as a governor of an energy-producing state, and kind of undo in my own area of expertise, and that's energy.

IFILL: So, Governor, as vice president, there's nothing that you have promised as a candidate that you would—that you wouldn't take off the table because of this financial crisis we're in?

PALIN: There is not. And how long have I been at this, like five weeks? So there hasn't been a whole lot that I've promised, except to do what is right for the American people, put government back on the side of the American people, stop the greed and corruption on Wall Street.

And the rescue plan has got to include that massive oversight that Americans are expecting and deserving. And I don't believe that John McCain has made any promise that he would not be able to keep, either.

IFILL: Senator?

BIDEN: Again, let me—let's talk about those tax breaks. Barack Obama—Obama voted for an energy bill because, for the first time, it had real support for alternative energy.

When there were separate votes on eliminating the tax breaks for the oil companies, Barack Obama voted to eliminate them. John did not.

And let me just ask a rhetorical question: If John really wanted to eliminate them, why is he adding to his budget an additional $4 billion in tax cuts for ExxonMobils of the world that, in fact, already have made $600 billion since 2001?

And, look, I agree with the governor. She imposed a windfall profits tax up there in Alaska. That's what Barack Obama and I want to do.

We want to be able to do for all of you Americans, give you back $1,000 bucks, like she's been able to give back money to her folks back there.

But John McCain will not support a windfall profits tax. They've made $600 billion since 2001, and John McCain wants to give them, all by itself—separate, no additional bill, all by itself—another $4 billion tax cut.

If that is not proof of what I say, I'm not sure what can be. So I hope the governor is able to convince John McCain to support our windfall profits tax, which she supported in Alaska, and I give her credit for it.

IFILL: Next question, Governor Palin, still on the economy. Last year, Congress passed a bill that would make it more difficult for debt-strapped mortgage-holders to declare bankruptcy, to get out from under that debt. This is something that John McCain supported. Would you have?

PALIN: Yes, I would have. But here, again, there have— there have been so many changes in the conditions of our economy in just even these past weeks that there has been more and more revelation made aware now to Americans about the corruption and the greed on Wall Street.

We need to look back, even two years ago, and we need to be appreciative of John McCain's call for reform with Fannie Mae, with Freddie Mac, with the mortgage-lenders, too, who were starting to really kind of rear that head of abuse.

And the colleagues in the Senate weren't going to go there with him. So we have John McCain to thank for at least warning people. And we also have John McCain to thank for bringing in a bipartisan effort people to the table so that we can start putting politics aside, even putting a campaign aside, and just do what's right to fix this economic problem that we are in.

It is a crisis. It's a toxic mess, really, on Main Street that's affecting Wall Street. And now we have to be ever vigilant and also making sure that credit markets don't seize up. That's where the Main Streeters like me, that's where we would really feel the effects.

IFILL: Senator Biden, you voted for this bankruptcy bill. Senator Obama voted against it. Some people have said that mortgage- holders really paid the price.

BIDEN: Well, mortgage-holders didn't pay the price. Only 10 percent of the people who are—have been affected by this whole switch from Chapter 7 to Chapter 13—it gets complicated.

But the point of this—Barack Obama saw the glass as half-empty. I saw it as half-full. We disagreed on that, and 85 senators voted one way, and 15 voted the other way.

But here's the deal. Barack Obama pointed out two years ago that there was a subprime mortgage crisis and wrote to the secretary of Treasury. And he said, "You'd better get on the stick here. You'd better look at it."

John McCain said as early as last December, quote—I'm paraphrasing—"I'm surprised about this subprime mortgage crisis," number one.

Number two, with regard to bankruptcy now, Gwen, what we should be doing now—and Barack Obama and I support it— we should be allowing bankruptcy courts to be able to readjust not just the interest rate you're paying on your mortgage to be able to stay in your home, but be able to adjust the principal that you owe, the principal that you owe.

That would keep people in their homes, actually help banks by keeping it from going under. But John McCain, as I understand it—I'm not sure of this, but I believe John McCain and the governor don't support that. There are ways to help people now. And there—ways that we're offering are not being supported by—by the Bush administration nor do I believe by John McCain and Governor Palin.

IFILL: Governor Palin, is that so?

PALIN: That is not so, but because that's just a quick answer, I want to talk about, again, my record on energy versus your ticket's energy ticket, also.

I think that this is important to come back to, with that energy policy plan again that was voted for in '05.

When we talk about energy, we have to consider the need to do all that we can to allow this nation to become energy independent.

It's a nonsensical position that we are in when we have domestic supplies of energy all over this great land. And East Coast politicians who don't allow energy-producing states like Alaska to produce these, to tap into them, and instead we're relying on foreign countries to produce for us.

PALIN: We're circulating about $700 billion a year into foreign countries, some who do not like America—they certainly don't have our best interests at heart—instead of those dollars circulating here, creating tens of thousands of

33

jobs and allowing domestic supplies of energy to be tapped into and start flowing into these very, very hungry markets.

Energy independence is the key to this nation's future, to our economic future, and to our national security. So when we talk about energy plans, it's not just about who got a tax break and who didn't. And we're not giving oil companies tax breaks, but it's about a heck of a lot more than that.

Energy independence is the key to America's future.

IFILL: Governor, I'm happy to talk to you in this next section about energy issues. Let's talk about climate change. What is true and what is false about what we have heard, read, discussed, debated about the causes of climate change?

PALIN: Yes. Well, as the nation's only Arctic state and being the governor of that state, Alaska feels and sees impacts of climate change more so than any other state. And we know that it's real.

I'm not one to attribute every man—activity of man to the changes in the climate. There is something to be said also for man's activities, but also for the cyclical temperature changes on our planet.

But there are real changes going on in our climate. And I don't want to argue about the causes. What I want to argue about is, how are we going to get there to positively affect the impacts?

We have got to clean up this planet. We have got to encourage other nations also to come along with us with the impacts of climate change, what we can do about that.

As governor, I was the first governor to form a climate change sub-cabinet to start dealing with the impacts. We've got to reduce emissions. John McCain is right there with an "all of the above" approach to deal with climate change impacts.

We've got to become energy independent for that reason. Also as we rely more and more on other countries that don't care as much about the climate as we do, we're allowing them to produce and to emit and even pollute more than America would ever stand for. So even in dealing with climate change, it's all the more reason that we have an "all of the above" approach, tapping into alternative sources of energy and conserving fuel, conserving our petroleum products and our hydrocarbons so that we can clean up this planet and deal with climate change.

IFILL: Senator, what is true and what is false about the causes?

BIDEN: Well, I think it is manmade. I think it's clearly manmade. And, look, this probably explains the biggest fundamental difference between John McCain and Barack Obama and Sarah Palin and Joe Biden—Governor Palin and Joe Biden.

If you don't understand what the cause is, it's virtually impossible to come up with a solution. We know what the cause is. The cause is manmade. That's the cause. That's why the polar icecap is melting.

Now, let's look at the facts. We have 3 percent of the world's oil reserves. We consume 25 percent of the oil in the world. John McCain has voted 20 times in the last decade-and-a-half against funding alternative energy sources, clean energy sources, wind, solar, biofuels.

The way in which we can stop the greenhouse gases from emitting. We believe—Barack Obama believes by investing in clean coal and safe nuclear, we can not only create jobs in wind and solar here in the United States, we can export it.

China is building one to three new coal-fired plants burning dirty coal per week. It's polluting not only the atmosphere but the West Coast of the United States. We should export the technology by investing in clean coal technology.

We should be creating jobs. John McCain has voted 20 times against funding alternative energy sources and thinks, I guess, the only answer is drill, drill, drill. Drill we must, but it will take 10 years for one drop of oil to come out of any of the wells that are going to begun to be drilled.

In the meantime, we're all going to be in real trouble.

IFILL: Let me clear something up, Senator McCain has said he supports caps on carbon emissions. Senator Obama has said he supports clean coal technology, which I don't believe you've always supported.

BIDEN: I have always supported it. That's a fact.

IFILL: Well, clear it up for us, both of you, and start with Governor Palin.

PALIN: Yes, Senator McCain does support this. The chant is "drill, baby, drill." And that's what we hear all across this country in our rallies because people are so hungry for those domestic sources of energy to be tapped into. They know that even in my own energy-producing state we have billions of barrels of oil and hundreds of trillions of cubic feet of clean, green natural gas. And we're building a nearly $40 billion natural gas pipeline which is North America's largest and most you expensive infrastructure project ever to flow those sources of energy into hungry markets.

Barack Obama and Senator Biden, you've said no to everything in trying to find a domestic solution to the energy crisis that we're in. You even called drilling—safe, environmentally-friendly drilling offshore as raping the outer continental shelf.

There—with new technology, with tiny footprints even on land, it is safe to drill and we need to do more of that. But also in that "all of the above" approach that Senator McCain supports, the alternative fuels will be tapped into: the nuclear, the clean coal.

I was surprised to hear you mention that because you had said that there isn't anything—such a thing as clean coal. And I think you said it in a rope line, too, at one of your rallies.

IFILL: We do need to keep within our two minutes. But I just wanted to ask you, do you support capping carbon emissions?

PALIN: I do. I do.

IFILL: OK. And on the clean coal issue?

BIDEN: Absolutely. Absolutely we do. We call for setting hard targets, number one...

IFILL: Clean coal.

BIDEN: Oh, I'm sorry.

IFILL: On clean coal.

BIDEN: Oh, on clean coal. My record, just take a look at the record. My record for 25 years has supported clean coal technology. A comment made in a rope line was taken out of context. I was talking about exporting that technology to China so when they burn their dirty coal, it won't be as dirty, it will be clean.

But here's the bottom line, Gwen: How do we deal with global warming with continued addition to carbon emissions? And if the only answer you have is oil, and John—and the governor says John is for everything.

Well, why did John vote 20 times? Maybe he's for everything as long as it's not helped forward by the government. Maybe he's for everything if the free market takes care of it. I don't know. But he voted 20 times against funding alternative energy sources.

IFILL: The next round of—pardon me, the next round of questions starts with you, Senator Biden. Do you support, as they do in Alaska, granting same-sex benefits to couples? **BIDEN:** Absolutely. Do I support granting same-sex benefits? Absolutely positively. Look, in an Obama-Biden administration, there will be absolutely no distinction from a constitutional standpoint or a legal standpoint between a same-sex and a heterosexual couple.

The fact of the matter is that under the Constitution we should be granted—same-sex couples should be able to have visitation rights in the hospitals, joint ownership of property, life insurance policies, et cetera. That's only fair.

It's what the Constitution calls for. And so we do support it. We do support making sure that committed couples in a same-sex marriage are guaranteed the same constitutional benefits as it relates to their property rights, their rights of visitation, their rights to insurance, their rights of ownership as heterosexual couples do.

IFILL: Governor, would you support expanding that beyond Alaska to the rest of the nation?

PALIN: Well, not if it goes closer and closer towards redefining the traditional definition of marriage between one man and one woman. And unfortunately that's sometimes where those steps lead.

But I also want to clarify, if there's any kind of suggestion at all from my answer that I would be anything but tolerant of adults in America choosing their partners, choosing relationships that they deem best for themselves, you know, I am tolerant and I have a very diverse family and group of friends and even within that group you would see some who may not agree with me on this issue, some very dear friends who don't agree with me on this issue.

But in that tolerance also, no one would ever propose, not in a McCain-Palin administration, to do anything to prohibit, say, visitations in a hospital or contracts being signed, negotiated between parties.

But I will tell Americans straight up that I don't support defining marriage as anything but between one man and one woman, and I think through nuances we can go round and round about what that actually means.

But I'm being as straight up with Americans as I can in my non- support for anything but a traditional definition of marriage.

IFILL: Let's try to avoid nuance, Senator. Do you support gay marriage?

BIDEN: No. Barack Obama nor I support redefining from a civil side what constitutes marriage. We do not support that. That is basically the decision to be able to be able to be left to faiths and people who practice their faiths the determination what you call it.

The bottom line though is, and I'm glad to hear the governor, I take her at her word, obviously, that she think there should be no civil rights distinction, none whatsoever, between a committed gay couple and a committed heterosexual couple. If that's the case, we really don't have a difference.

IFILL: Is that what your said?

PALIN: Your question to him was whether he supported gay marriage and my answer is the same as his and it is that I do not.

IFILL: Wonderful. You agree. On that note, let's move to foreign policy.

IFILL: You both have sons who are in Iraq or on their way to Iraq. You, Governor Palin, have said that you would like to see a real clear plan for an exit strategy. What should that be, Governor?

PALIN: I am very thankful that we do have a good plan and the surge and the counterinsurgency strategy in Iraq that has proven to work, I am thankful that that is part of the plan implemented under a great American hero, General Petraeus, and pushed hard by another great American, Senator John McCain.

I know that the other ticket opposed this surge, in fact, even opposed funding for our troops in Iraq and Afghanistan. Barack Obama voted against funding troops there after promising that he would not do so.

PALIN: And Senator Biden, I respected you when you called him out on that. You said that his vote was political and you said it would cost lives. And Barack Obama at first said he would not do that. He turned around under political pressure and he voted against funding the troops. We do have a plan for withdrawal. We don't need early withdrawal out of Iraq. We cannot afford to lose there or we're going to be no better off in the war in Afghanistan either. We have got to win in Iraq.

And with the surge that has worked we're now down to pre-surge numbers in Iraq. That's where we can be. We can start putting more troops in Afghanistan as we also work with our NATO allies who are there strengthening us and we need to grow our military. We cannot afford to lose against al Qaeda and the Shia extremists who are still there, still fighting us, but we're getting closer and closer to victory. And it would be a travesty if we quit now in Iraq.

IFILL: Senator?

BIDEN: Gwen, with all due respect, I didn't hear a plan. Barack Obama offered a clear plan. Shift responsibility to Iraqis over the next 16 months. Draw down our combat troops. Ironically the same plan that Maliki, the prime minister of Iraq and George Bush are now negotiating. The only odd man out here, only one left out is John McCain, number one. Number two, with regard to Barack Obama not quote funding the troops, John McCain voted the exact same way. John McCain voted against funding the troops because of an amendment he voted against had a timeline in it to draw down American troops. And John said I'm not going to fund the troops if in fact there's a time line. Barack Obama and I agree fully and completely on one thing. You've got to have a time line to draw down the troops and shift responsibility to the Iraqis.

We're spending $10 billion a month while Iraqis have an $80 billion surplus. Barack says it's time for them to spend their own money and have the 400,000 military we trained for them begin to take their own responsibility and gradually over 16 months, withdrawal. John McCain—this is a fundamental difference between us, we'll end this war. For John McCain, there's no end in sight to end this war, fundamental difference. We will end this war.

IFILL: Governor?

PALIN: Your plan is a white flag of surrender in Iraq and that is not what our troops need to hear today, that's for sure. And it's not what our nation needs to be able to count on. You guys opposed the surge. The surge worked. Barack Obama still can't admit the surge works.

We'll know when we're finished in Iraq when the Iraqi government can govern its people and when the Iraqi security forces can secure its people. And our commanders on the ground will tell us when those conditions have been met. And Maliki and Talabani also in working with us are knowing again that we are getting closer and closer to that point, that victory that's within sight.

Now, you said regarding Senator McCain's military policies there, Senator Biden, that you supported a lot of these things. In fact, you said in fact that you wanted to run, you'd be honored to run with him on the ticket. That's an indication I think of some of the support that you had at least until you became the VP pick here.

You also said that Barack Obama was not ready to be commander in chief. And I know again that you opposed the move he made to try to cut off funding for the troops and I respect you for that. I don't know how you can defend that position now but I know that you know especially with your son in the National Guard and I have great respect for your family also and the honor that you show our military. Barack Obama though, another story there. Anyone I think who can cut off funding for the troops after promising not to is another story.

IFILL: Senator Biden?

BIDEN: John McCain voted to cut off funding for the troops. Let me say that again. John McCain voted against an amendment containing $1 billion, $600 million that I had gotten to get MRAPS, those things that are protecting the governor's son and pray god my son and a lot of other sons and daughters.

He voted against it. He voted against funding because he said the amendment had a time line in it to end this war. He didn't like that. But let's get straight who has been right and wrong. John McCain and Dick Cheney said while I was saying we would not be greeted as liberators, we would not—

this war would take a decade and not a day, not a week and not six months, we would not be out of there quickly. John McCain was saying the Sunnis and Shias got along with each other without reading the history of the last 700 years. John McCain said there would be enough oil to pay for this. John McCain has been dead wrong. I love him. As my mother would say, god love him, but he's been dead wrong on the fundamental issues relating to the conduct of the war. Barack Obama has been right. There are the facts.

IFILL: Let's move to Iran and Pakistan. I'm curious about what you think starting with you Senator Biden. What's the greater threat, a nuclear Iran or an unstable Afghanistan? Explain why.

BIDEN: Well, they're both extremely dangerous. I always am focused, as you know Gwen, I have been focusing on for a long time, along with Barack on Pakistan. Pakistan already has nuclear weapons. Pakistan already has deployed nuclear weapons. Pakistan's weapons can already hit Israel and the Mediterranean. Iran getting a nuclear weapon would be very, very destabilizing. They are more than—they are not close to getting a nuclear weapon that's able to be deployed. So they're both very dangerous. They both would be game changers.

But look, here's what the fundamental problem I have with John's policy about terror instability. John continues to tell us that the central war in the front on terror is in Iraq. I promise you, if an attack comes in the homeland, it's going to come as our security services have said, it is going to come from al Qaeda planning in the hills of Afghanistan and Pakistan. That's where they live. That's where they are. That's where it will come from. And right now that resides in Pakistan, a stable government needs to be established. We need to support that democracy by helping them not only with their military but with their governance and their economic well-being.

There have been 7,000 madrasses built along that border. We should be helping them build schools to compete for those hearts and minds of the people in the region so that we're actually able to take on terrorism and by the way, that's where bin Laden lives and we will go at him if we have actionable intelligence.

IFILL: Governor, nuclear Pakistan, unstable Pakistan, nuclear Iran? Which is the greater threat?

PALIN: Both are extremely dangerous, of course. And as for who coined that central war on terror being in Iraq, it was the General Petraeus and al Qaeda, both leaders there and it's probably the only thing that they're ever going to agree on, but that it was a central war on terror is in Iraq. You don't have to believe me or John McCain on that. I would believe Petraeus and the leader of al Qaeda.

An armed, nuclear armed especially Iran is so extremely dangerous to consider. They cannot be allowed to acquire nuclear weapons period. Israel is in jeopardy of course when we're dealing with Ahmadinejad as a leader of Iran. Iran claiming that Israel as he termed it, a stinking corpse, a country that should be wiped off the face of the earth. Now a leader like Ahmadinejad who is not sane or stable when he says things like that is not one whom we can allow to acquire nuclear energy, nuclear weapons. Ahmadinejad, Kim Jong Il, the Castro brothers, others who are dangerous dictators are one that Barack Obama has said he would be willing to meet with without preconditions being met first.

45

And an issue like that taken up by a presidential candidate goes beyond naiveté and goes beyond poor judgment. A statement that he made like that is downright dangerous because leaders like Ahmadinejad who would seek to acquire nuclear weapons and wipe off the face of the earth an ally like we have in Israel should not be met with without preconditions and diplomatic efforts being undertaken first.

IFILL: Governor and senator, I want you both to respond to this. Secretaries of state Baker, Kissinger, Powell, they have all advocated some level of engagement with enemies. Do you think these former secretaries of state are wrong on that?

PALIN: No and Dr. Henry Kissinger especially. I had a good conversation with him recently. And he shared with me his passion for diplomacy. And that's what John McCain and I would engage in also. But again, with some of these dictators who hate America and hate what we stand for, with our freedoms, our democracy, our tolerance, our respect for women's rights, those who would try to destroy what we stand for cannot be met with just sitting down on a presidential level as Barack Obama had said he would be willing to do. That is beyond bad judgment. That is dangerous.

No, diplomacy is very important. First and foremost, that is what we would engage in. But diplomacy is hard work by serious people. It's lining out clear objectives and having your friends and your allies ready to back you up there and have sanctions lined up before any kind of presidential summit would take place.

IFILL: Senator?

BIDEN: Can I clarify this? This is simply not true about Barack Obama. He did not say sit down with Ahmadinejad.

BIDEN: The fact of the matter is, it surprises me that Senator McCain doesn't realize that Ahmadinejad does not control the security apparatus in Iran. The theocracy controls the security apparatus, number one.

Number two, five secretaries of state did say we should talk with and sit down.

Now, John and Governor Palin now say they're all for—they have a passion, I think the phrase was, a passion for diplomacy and that we have to bring our friends and allies along.

Our friends and allies have been saying, Gwen, "Sit down. Talk. Talk. Talk." Our friends and allies have been saying that, five secretaries of state, three of them Republicans.

And John McCain has said he would go along with an agreement, but he wouldn't sit down. Now, how do you do that when you don't have your administration sit down and talk with the adversary?

And look what President Bush did. After five years, he finally sent a high-ranking diplomat to meet with the highest-ranking diplomats in Iran, in Europe, to try to work out an arrangement.

Our allies are on that same page. And if we don't go the extra mile on diplomacy, what makes you think the allies are going to sit with us?

The last point I'll make, John McCain said as recently as a couple of weeks ago he wouldn't even sit down with the government of Spain, a NATO ally that has troops in Afghanistan with us now. I find that incredible.

IFILL: Governor, you mentioned Israel and your support for Israel.

PALIN: Yes.

IFILL: What has this administration done right or wrong— this is the great, lingering, unresolved issue, the Israeli-Palestinian conflict—what have they done? And is a two-state solution the solution?

PALIN: A two-state solution is the solution. And Secretary Rice, having recently met with leaders on one side or the other there, also, still in these waning days of the Bush administration, trying to forge that peace, and that needs to be done, and that will be top of an agenda item, also, under a McCain-Palin administration.

Israel is our strongest and best ally in the Middle East. We have got to assure them that we will never allow a second Holocaust, despite, again, warnings from Iran and any other country that would seek to destroy Israel, that that is what they would like to see.

We will support Israel. A two-state solution, building our embassy, also, in Jerusalem, those things that we look forward to being able to accomplish, with this peace-seeking nation, and they have a track record of being able to forge these peace agreements.

They succeeded with Jordan. They succeeded with Egypt. I'm sure that we're going to see more success there, also.

It's got to be a commitment of the United States of America, though. And I can promise you, in a McCain-Palin administration, that commitment is there to work with our friends in Israel.

IFILL: Senator?

BIDEN: Gwen, no one in the United States Senate has been a better friend to Israel than Joe Biden. I would have never, ever joined this ticket were I not absolutely sure Barack Obama shared my passion.

But you asked a question about whether or not this administration's policy had made sense or something to that effect. It has been an abject failure, this administration's policy.

In fairness to Secretary Rice, she's trying to turn it around now in the seventh or eighth year.

Here's what the president said when we said no. He insisted on elections on the West Bank, when I said, and others said, and Barack Obama said, "Big mistake. Hamas will win. You'll legitimize them." What happened? Hamas won.

When we kicked—along with France, we kicked Hezbollah out of Lebanon, I said and Barack said, "Move NATO forces in there. Fill the vacuum, because if you don't know—if you don't, Hezbollah will control it."

Now what's happened? Hezbollah is a legitimate part of the government in the country immediately to the north of Israel.

The fact of the matter is, the policy of this administration has been an abject failure.

And speaking of freedom being on the march, the only thing on the march is Iran. It's closer to a bomb. Its proxies now have a major stake in Lebanon, as well as in the Gaza Strip with Hamas.

We will change this policy with thoughtful, real, live diplomacy that understands that you must back Israel in letting them negotiate, support their negotiation, and stand with them, not insist on policies like this administration has. IFILL: Has this administration's policy been an abject failure, as the senator says, Governor?

PALIN: No, I do not believe that it has been. But I'm so encouraged to know that we both love Israel, and I think that is a good thing to get to agree on, Senator Biden. I respect your position on that.

No, in fact, when we talk about the Bush administration, there's a time, too, when Americans are going to say, "Enough is enough with your ticket," on constantly looking backwards, and pointing fingers, and doing the blame game.

There have been huge blunders in the war. There have been huge blunders throughout this administration, as there are with every administration.

But for a ticket that wants to talk about change and looking into the future, there's just too much finger-pointing backwards to ever make us believe that that's where you're going.

Positive change is coming, though. Reform of government is coming. We'll learn from the past mistakes in this administration and other administrations.

And we're going to forge ahead with putting government back on the side of the people and making sure that our country comes first, putting obsessive partisanship aside.

That's what John McCain has been known for in all these years. He has been the maverick. He has ruffled feathers.

But I know, Senator Biden, you have respected for them that, and I respect you for acknowledging that. But change is coming.

IFILL: Just looking backwards, Senator?

BIDEN: Look, past is prologue, Gwen. The issue is, how different is John McCain's policy going to be than George Bush's? I haven't heard anything yet.

I haven't heard how his policy is going to be different on Iran than George Bush's. I haven't heard how his policy is going to be different with Israel than George Bush's. I haven't heard how his policy in Afghanistan is going to be different than George Bush's. I haven't heard how his policy in Pakistan is going to be different than George Bush's.

It may be. But so far, it is the same as George Bush's. And you know where that policy has taken us.

We will make significant change so, once again, we're the most respected nation in the world. That's what we're going to do.

IFILL: Governor, on another issue, interventionism, nuclear weapons. What should be the trigger, or should there be a trigger, when nuclear weapons use is ever put into play?

PALIN: Nuclear weaponry, of course, would be the be all, end all of just too many people in too many parts of our planet, so those dangerous regimes, again, cannot be allowed to acquire nuclear weapons, period.

Our nuclear weaponry here in the U.S. is used as a deterrent. And that's a safe, stable way to use nuclear weaponry.

But for those countries—North Korea, also, under Kim Jong-il—we have got to make sure that we're putting the economic sanctions on these countries and that we have friends and allies supporting us in this to make sure that leaders like Kim Jong-il and Ahmadinejad are not allowed to acquire, to proliferate, or to use those nuclear weapons. It is that important.

Can we talk about Afghanistan real quick, also, though?

IFILL: Certainly.

PALIN: OK, I'd like to just really quickly mention there, too, that when you look back and you say that the Bush administration's policy on Afghanistan perhaps would be the same as McCain, and that's not accurate.

The surge principles, not the exact strategy, but the surge principles that have worked in Iraq need to be implemented in Afghanistan, also. And that, perhaps, would be a difference with the Bush administration.

Now, Barack Obama had said that all we're doing in Afghanistan is air-raiding villages and killing civilians. And such a reckless, reckless comment and untrue comment, again, hurts our cause.

That's not what we're doing there. We're fighting terrorists, and we're securing democracy, and we're building schools for children there so that there is opportunity in that country, also. There will be a big difference there, and we will win in— in Afghanistan, also.

IFILL: Senator, you may talk about nuclear use, if you'd like, and also about Afghanistan.

BIDEN: I'll talk about both. With Afghanistan, facts matter, Gwen.

The fact is that our commanding general in Afghanistan said today that a surge—the surge principles used in Iraq will not—well, let me say this again now—our commanding general in Afghanistan said the surge principle in Iraq will not work in Afghanistan, not Joe Biden, our commanding general in Afghanistan.

He said we need more troops. We need government-building. We need to spend more money on the infrastructure in Afghanistan.

Look, we have spent more money—we spend more money in three weeks on combat in Iraq than we spent on the entirety of the last seven years that we have been in Afghanistan building that country.

Let me say that again. Three weeks in Iraq; seven years, seven years or six-and-a-half years in Afghanistan. Now, that's number one.

Number two, with regard to arms control and weapons, nuclear weapons require a nuclear arms control regime. John McCain voted against a Comprehensive Nuclear-Test-Ban Treaty that every Republican has supported.

John McCain has opposed amending the Nuclear-Test-Ban Treaty with an amendment to allow for inspections.

John McCain has not been—has not been the kind of supporter for dealing with—and let me put it another way. My time is almost up.

Barack Obama, first thing he did when he came to the United States Senate, new senator, reached across the aisle to my colleague, Dick Lugar, a Republican, and said, "We've got to do something about keeping nuclear weapons out of the hands of terrorists."

They put together a piece of legislation that, in fact, was serious and real. Every major—I shouldn't say every—on the two at least that I named, I know that John McCain has been opposed to extending the arms control regime in the world.

IFILL: Governor?

PALIN: Well, first, McClellan did not say definitively the surge principles would not work in Afghanistan. Certainly, accounting for different conditions in that different country and conditions are certainly different. We have NATO allies helping us for one and even the geographic differences are huge but the counterinsurgency principles could work in

Afghanistan. McClellan didn't say anything opposite of that. The counterinsurgency strategy going into Afghanistan, clearing, holding, rebuilding, the civil society and the infrastructure can work in Afghanistan. And those leaders who are over there, who have also been advising George Bush on this have not said anything different but that.

IFILL: Senator.

BIDEN: Well, our commanding general did say that. The fact of the matter is that again, I'll just put in perspective, while Barack and I and Chuck Hagel and Dick Lugar have been calling for more money to help in Afghanistan, more troops in Afghanistan, John McCain was saying two years ago quote, "The reason we don't read about Afghanistan anymore in the paper, it's succeeded.

Barack Obama was saying we need more troops there. Again, we spend in three weeks on combat missions in Iraq, more than we spent in the entire time we have been in Afghanistan. That will change in a Barack Obama administration.

IFILL: Senator, you have quite a record, this is the next question here, of being an interventionist. You argued for intervention in Bosnia and Kosovo, initially in Iraq and Pakistan and now in Darfur, putting U.S. troops on the ground. Boots on the ground. Is this something the American public has the stomach for?

BIDEN: I think the American public has the stomach for success. My recommendations on Bosnia. I admit I was the first one to recommend it. They saved tens of thousands of lives. And initially John McCain opposed it along with a lot of other people. But the end result was it worked. Look what we did in Bosnia. We took Serbs, Croats and Bosniaks, being told by everyone, I was told by everyone that this would mean that they had been killing each other for a thousand years, it would never work.

There's a relatively stable government there now as in Kosovo. With regard to Iraq, I indicated it would be a mistake to—I gave the president the power. I voted for the power because he said he needed it not to go to war but to keep the United States, the UN in line, to keep sanctions on Iraq and not let them be lifted.

I, along with Dick Lugar, before we went to war, said if we were to go to war without our allies, without the kind of support we need, we'd be there for a decade and it'd cost us tens of billions of dollars. John McCain said, no, it was going to be OK.

I don't have the stomach for genocide when it comes to Darfur. We can now impose a no-fly zone. It's within our capacity. We can lead NATO if we're willing to take a hard stand. We can, I've been in those camps in Chad. I've seen the suffering, thousands and tens of thousands have died and are dying. We should rally the world to act and demonstrate it by our own movement to provide the helicopters to get the 21,000 forces of the African Union in there now to stop this genocide.

IFILL: Thank you, senator. Governor.

PALIN: Oh, yeah, it's so obvious I'm a Washington outsider. And someone just not used to the way you guys operate. Because here you voted for the war and now you oppose the war. You're one who says, as so many politicians do, I was for it before I was against it or vice- versa. Americans are craving that straight talk and just want to know, hey, if you voted for it, tell us why you voted for it and it was a war resolution.

And you had supported John McCain's military strategies pretty adamantly until this race and you had opposed very adamantly Barack Obama's military strategy, including cutting off funding for the troops that attempt all through the primary.

And I watched those debates, so I remember what those were all about.

But as for Darfur, we can agree on that also, the supported of the no-fly zone, making sure that all options are on the table there also.

America is in a position to help. What I've done in my position to help, as the governor of a state that's pretty rich in natural resources, we have a $40 billion investment fund, a savings fund called the Alaska Permanent Fund.

When I and others in the legislature found out we had some millions of dollars in Sudan, we called for divestment through legislation of those dollars to make sure we weren't doing anything that would be seen as condoning the activities there in Darfur. That legislation hasn't passed yet but it needs to because all of us, as individuals, and as humanitarians and as elected officials should do all we can to end those atrocities in that region of the world.

IFILL: Is there a line that should be drawn about when we decide to go in?

BIDEN: Absolutely. There is a line that should be drawn.

IFILL: What is it? BIDEN: The line that should be drawn is whether we A, first of all have the capacity to do anything about it number one. And number two, certain new lines that have to be drawn internationally. When a country engages in genocide, when a country engaging in harboring terrorists and will do nothing about it, at that point that country in my view and Barack's view forfeits their right to say you have no right to intervene at all.

The truth of the matter is, though, let's go back to John McCain's strategy. I never supported John McCain's strategy on the war. John McCain said exactly what Dick Cheney said, go back and look at Barack Obama's statements and mine. Go look at joebiden.com, contemporaneously, held hearings in the summer before we went to war, saying if we went to war, we would not be greeted as liberator, we would have a fight between Sunnis and Shias, we would be tied down for a decade and cost us hundreds of billions of dollars.

John McCain was saying the exact opposite. John McCain was lock- step with Dick Cheney at that point how this was going to be easy. So John McCain's strategy in this war, not just whether or not to go, the actual conduct of the war has been absolutely wrong from the outset.

IFILL: Governor.

PALIN: I beg to disagree with you, again, here on whether you supported Barack Obama or John McCain's strategies. Here again, you can say what you want to say a month out before people are asked to vote on this, but we listened to the debates.

I think tomorrow morning, the pundits are going to start do the who said what at what time and we'll have proof of some of this, but, again, John McCain who knows how to win a war. Who's been there and he's faced challenges and he knows what evil is and knows what it takes to overcome the challenges here with our military.

He knows to learn from the mistakes and blunders we have seen in the war in Iraq, especially. He will know how to implement the strategies, working with our commanders and listening to what they have to say, taking the politics out of these war issues. He'll know how to win a war.

IFILL: Thank you, governor.

Probably the biggest cliche about the vice-presidency is that it's a heartbeat away, everybody's waiting to see what would happen if the worst happened. How would—you disagree on some things from your principles, you disagree on drilling in Alaska, the National Wildlife Refuge, you disagree on the surveillance law, at least you have in the past. How would a Biden administration be different from an Obama administration if that were to happen.

BIDEN: God forbid that would ever happen, it would be a national tragedy of historic proportions if it were to happen.

But if it did, I would carry out Barack Obama's policy, his policies of reinstating the middle class, making sure they get a fair break, making sure they have access to affordable health insurance, making sure they get serious tax breaks, making sure we can help their children get to college, making sure there is an energy policy that leads us in the direction of not only toward independence and clean environment but an energy policy that creates 5 million new jobs, a foreign policy that ends this war in Iraq, a foreign policy that goes after the one mission the American public gave the president after

9/11, to get and capture or kill bin Laden and to eliminate al Qaeda. A policy that would in fact engage our allies in making sure that we knew we were acting on the same page and not dictating.

And a policy that would reject the Bush Doctrine of preemption and regime change and replace it with a doctrine of prevention and cooperation and, ladies and gentlemen, this is the biggest ticket item that we have in this election.

This is the most important election you will ever, ever have voted in, any of you, since 1932. And there's such stark differences, I would follow through on Barack's policies because in essence, I agree with every major initiative he is suggesting.

IFILL: Governor.

PALIN: And heaven forbid, yes, that would ever happen, no matter how this ends up, that that would ever happen with either party.

As for disagreeing with John McCain and how our administration would work, what do you expect? A team of mavericks, of course we're not going to agree on 100 percent of everything. As we discuss ANWR there, at least we can agree to disagree on that one. I will keep pushing him on ANWR. I have so appreciated he has never asked me to check my opinions at the door and he wants a deliberative debate and healthy debate so we can make good policy.

What I would do also, if that were to ever happen, though, is to continue the good work he is so committed to of putting government back on the side of the people and get rid of the greed and corruption on Wall Street and in Washington.

I think we need a little bit of reality from Wasilla Main Street there, brought to Washington, DC.

PALIN: So that people there can understand how the average working class family is viewing bureaucracy in the federal government and Congress and inaction of Congress.

Just everyday working class Americans saying, you know, government, just get out of my way. If you're going to do any harm and mandate more things on me and take more of my money and income tax and business taxes, you're going to have a choice in just a few weeks here on either supporting a ticket that wants to create jobs and bolster our economy and win the war or you're going to be supporting a ticket that wants to increase taxes, which ultimately kills jobs, and is going to hurt our economy.

BIDEN: Can I respond? Look, all you have to do is go down Union Street with me in Wilmington or go to Katie's Restaurant or walk into Home Depot with me where I spend a lot of time and you ask anybody in there whether or not the economic and foreign policy of this administration has made them better off in the last eight years. And then ask them whether there's a single major initiative that John McCain differs with the president on. On taxes, on Iraq, on Afghanistan, on the whole question of how to help education, on the dealing with health care.

Look, the people in my neighborhood, they get it. They get it. They know they've been getting the short end of the stick. So walk with me in my neighborhood, go back to my old neighborhood in Claymont, an old steel town or go up to Scranton with me. These people know the middle class has gotten the short end. The wealthy have done very well.

Corporate America has been rewarded. It's time we change it. Barack Obama will change it.

IFILL: Governor?

PALIN: Say it ain't so, Joe, there you go again pointing backwards again. You preferenced your whole comment with the Bush administration. Now doggone it, let's look ahead and tell Americans what we have to plan to do for them in the future. You mentioned education and I'm glad you did. I know education you are passionate about with your wife being a teacher for 30 years, and god bless her. Her reward is in heaven, right? I say, too, with education, America needs to be putting a lot more focus on that and our schools have got to be really ramped up in terms of the funding that they are deserving. Teachers needed to be paid more. I come from a house full of school teachers. My grandma was, my dad who is in the audience today, he's a schoolteacher, had been for many years. My brother, who I think is the best schoolteacher in the year, and here's a shout-out to all those third graders at Gladys Wood Elementary School, you get extra credit for watching the debate.

Education credit in American has been in some sense in some of our states just accepted to be a little bit lax and we have got to increase the standards. No Child Left Behind was implemented. It's not doing the job though. We need flexibility in No Child Left Behind. We need to put more of an emphasis on the profession of teaching. We need to make sure that education in either one of our agendas, I think, absolute top of the line. My kids as public school participants right now, it's near and dear to my heart. I'm very, very concerned about where we're going with education and we have got to ramp it up and put more attention in that arena.

IFILL: Everybody gets extra credit tonight. We're going to move on to the next question. Governor, you said in July that someone would have to explain to you exactly what it is the vice president does every day. You, senator, said, you would not be vice president under any circumstances. Now maybe this was just what was going on at the time. But tell us now, looking forward, what it is you think the vice presidency is worth now.

PALIN: In my comment there, it was a lame attempt at a joke and yours was a lame attempt at a joke, too, I guess, because nobody got it. Of course we know what a vice president does.

BIDEN: They didn't get yours or mine? Which one didn't they get?

PALIN: No, no. Of course, we know what a vice president does. And that's not only to preside over the Senate and will take that position very seriously also. I'm thankful the Constitution would allow a bit more authority given to the vice president if that vice president so chose to exert it in working with the Senate and making sure that we are supportive of the president's policies and making sure too that our president understands what our strengths are. John McCain and I have had good conversations about where I would lead with his agenda. That is energy independence in America and reform of government over all, and then working with families of children with special needs. That's near and dear to my heart also. In those arenas, John McCain has already tapped me and said, that's where I want you, I want you to lead. I said, I can't wait to get and there go to work with you.

IFILL: Senator?

BIDEN: Gwen, I hope we'll get back to education because I don't know any government program that John is supporting, not early education, more money for it. The reason No Child Left Behind was left behind, the money was left behind, we didn't fund it. We can get back to that I assume.

With regard to the role of vice president, I had a long talk, as I'm sure the governor did with her principal, in my case with Barack. Let me tell you what Barack asked me to do. I have a history of getting things done in the United States Senate. John McCain would acknowledge that. My record shows that on controversial issues. I would be the point person for the legislative initiatives in the United States Congress for our administration. I would also, when asked if I wanted a portfolio, my response was, no. But Barack Obama indicated to me he wanted me with him to help him govern. So every major decision he'll be making, I'll be sitting in the room to give my best advice. He's president, not me, I'll give my best advice.

And one of the things he said early on when he was choosing, he said he picked someone who had an independent judgment and wouldn't be afraid to tell him if he disagreed. That is sort of my reputation, as you know. I look forward to working with Barack and playing a very constructive role in his presidency, bringing about the kind of change this country needs.

IFILL: Governor, you mentioned a moment ago the constitution might give the vice president more power than it has in the past. Do you believe as Vice President Cheney does, that the Executive Branch does not hold complete sway over the office of the vice presidency, that it it is also a member of the Legislative Branch?

PALIN: Well, our founding fathers were very wise there in allowing through the Constitution much flexibility there in the office of the vice president. And we will do what is best for the American people in tapping into that position and ushering in an agenda that is supportive and cooperative with the president's agenda in that position. Yeah, so I do agree with him that we have a lot of flexibility in there, and we'll do what we have to do to administer very appropriately the plans that are needed for this nation. And it is my executive experience that is partly to be attributed to my pick as V.P. with McCain, not only as a governor, but earlier on as a mayor, as an oil and gas regulator, as a business owner. It is those years of experience on an executive level that will be put to good use in the White House also.

IFILL: Vice President Cheney's interpretation of the vice presidency?

BIDEN: Vice President Cheney has been the most dangerous vice president we've had probably in American history. The idea he doesn't realize that Article I of the Constitution defines the role of the vice president of the United States, that's the Executive Branch. He works in the Executive Branch. He should understand that. Everyone should understand that.

And the primary role of the vice president of the United States of America is to support the president of the United States of America, give that president his or her best judgment when sought, and as vice president, to preside over the Senate, only in a time when in fact there's a tie vote. The Constitution is explicit.

The only authority the vice president has from the legislative standpoint is the vote, only when there is a tie vote. He has no authority relative to the Congress. The idea he's part of the Legislative Branch is a bizarre notion invented by Cheney to aggrandize the power of a unitary executive and look where it has gotten us. It has been very dangerous. IFILL: Let's talk conventional wisdom for a moment. The conventional wisdom, Governor Palin with you, is that your Achilles heel is that you lack experience. Your conventional wisdom against you is that your Achilles heel is that you lack discipline, Senator Biden. What id it really for you, Governor Palin? What is it really for you, Senator Biden? Start with you, governor.

PALIN: My experience as an executive will be put to good use as a mayor and business owner and oil and gas regulator and then as governor of a huge state, a huge energy producing state that is accounting for much progress towards getting our nation energy independence and that's extremely important.

But it wasn't just that experience tapped into, it was my connection to the heartland of America. Being a mom, one very concerned about a son in the war, about a special needs child, about kids heading off to college, how are we going to pay those tuition bills? About times and Todd and our marriage in our past where we didn't have health insurance and we know what other Americans are going through as they sit around the kitchen table and try to figure out how are they going to pay out-of-pocket for health care? We've been there also so that connection was important.

But even more important is that world view that I share with John McCain. That world view that says that America is a nation of exceptionalism. And we are to be that shining city on a hill, as President Reagan so beautifully said, that we are a beacon of hope and that we are unapologetic here. We are not perfect as a nation. But together, we represent a perfect ideal. And that is democracy and tolerance and freedom and equal rights. Those things that we stand for that can be put to good use as a force for good in this world.

John McCain and I share that. You combine all that with being a team with the only track record of making a really, a difference in where we've been and reforming, that's a good team, it's a good ticket.

IFILL: Senator?

BIDEN: You're very kind suggesting my only Achilles Heel is my lack of discipline.

BIDEN: Others talk about my excessive passion. I'm not going to change. I have 35 years in public office. People can judge who I am. I haven't changed in that time.

And, by the way, a record of change—I will place my record and Barack's record against John McCain's or anyone else in terms of fundamental accomplishments. Wrote the crime bill, put 100,000 cops on the street, wrote the Violence Against Women Act, which John McCain voted against both of them, was the catalyst to change the circumstance in Bosnia, led by President Clinton, obviously.

Look, I understand what it's like to be a single parent. When my wife and daughter died and my two sons were gravely injured, I understand what it's like as a parent to wonder what it's like if your kid's going to make it.

I understand what it's like to sit around the kitchen table with a father who says, "I've got to leave, champ, because there's no jobs here. I got to head down to Wilmington. And when we get enough money, honey, we'll bring you down."

I understand what it's like. I'm much better off than almost all Americans now. I get a good salary with the United States Senate. I live in a beautiful house that's my total investment that I have. So I—I am much better off now.

But the notion that somehow, because I'm a man, I don't know what it's like to raise two kids alone, I don't know what it's like to have a child you're not sure is going to—is going to make it—I understand.

I understand, as well as, with all due respect, the governor or anybody else, what it's like for those people sitting around that kitchen table. And guess what? They're looking for help. They're looking for help. They're not looking for more of the same.

IFILL: Governor?

PALIN: People aren't looking for more of the same. They are looking for change. And John McCain has been the consummate maverick in the Senate over all these years.

He's taken shots left and right from the other party and from within his own party, because he's had to take on his own party when the time was right, when he recognized it was time to put partisanship aside and just do what was right for the American people. That's what I've done as governor, also, take on my own party, when I had to, and work with both sides of the aisle, in my cabinet, appointing those who would serve regardless of party, Democrats, independents, Republicans, whatever it took to get the job done.

Also, John McCain's maverick position that he's in, that's really prompt up to and indicated by the supporters that he has. Look at Lieberman, and Giuliani, and Romney, and Lingle, and all of us who come from such a diverse background of—of policy and of partisanship, all coming together at this time, recognizing he is the man that we need to leave—lead in these next four years, because these are tumultuous times.

We have got to win the wars. We have got to get our economy back on track. We have got to not allow the greed and corruption on Wall Street anymore.

And we have not got to allow the partisanship that has really been entrenched in Washington, D.C., no matter who's been in charge. When the Republicans were in charge, I didn't see a lot of progress there, either. When the Democrats, either, though, this last go- around for the last two years.

Change is coming. And John McCain is the leader of that reform.

IFILL: Senator...

BIDEN: I'll be very brief. Can I respond to that?

Look, the maverick—let's talk about the maverick John McCain is. And, again, I love him. He's been a maverick on some issues, but he has been no maverick on the things that matter to people's lives.

He voted four out of five times for George Bush's budget, which put us a half a trillion dollars in debt this year and over $3 trillion in debt since he's got there.

He has not been a maverick in providing health care for people. He has voted against—he voted including another 3.6 million children in coverage of the existing health care plan, when he voted in the United States Senate.

He's not been a maverick when it comes to education. He has not supported tax cuts and significant changes for people being able to send their kids to college.

He's not been a maverick on the war. He's not been a maverick on virtually anything that genuinely affects the things that people really talk about around their kitchen table.

Can we send—can we get Mom's MRI? Can we send Mary back to school next semester? We can't—we can't make it. How are we going to heat the—heat the house this winter?

He voted against even providing for what they call LIHEAP, for assistance to people, with oil prices going through the roof in the winter.

So maverick he is not on the important, critical issues that affect people at that kitchen table.

IFILL: Final question tonight, before your closing statements, starting with you, Senator Biden. Can you think of a single issue—and this is to cast light for people who are just trying to get to know you in your final debate, your only debate of this year—can you think of a single issue, policy issue, in which you were forced to change a long-held view in order to accommodate changed circumstances?

BIDEN: Yes, I can. When I got to the United States Senate and went on the Judiciary Committee as a young lawyer, I was of the view and had been trained in the view that the only thing that mattered was whether or not a nominee appointed, suggested by the president had a judicial temperament, had not committed a crime of moral turpitude, and was—had been a good student.

And it didn't take me long—it was hard to change, but it didn't take me long, but it took about five years for me to realize that the ideology of that judge makes a big difference.

That's why I led the fight against Judge Bork. Had he been on the court, I suspect there would be a lot of changes that I don't like and the American people wouldn't like, including everything from Roe v. Wade to issues relating to civil rights and civil liberties.

And so that—that—that was one of the intellectual changes that took place in my career as I got a close look at it. And that's why I was the first chairman of the Judiciary Committee to forthrightly state that it matters what your judicial philosophy is. The American people have a right to understand it and to know it.

But I did change on that, and—and I'm glad I did.

IFILL: Governor?

PALIN: There have been times where, as mayor and governor, we have passed budgets that I did not veto and that I think could be considered as something that I quasi-caved in, if you will, but knowing that it was the right thing to do in order to progress the agenda for that year and to work with the legislative body, that body that actually holds the purse strings.

So there were times when I wanted to zero-base budget, and to cut taxes even more, and I didn't have enough support in order to accomplish that.

But on the major principle things, no, there hasn't been something that I've had to compromise on, because we've always seemed to find a way to work together. Up there in Alaska, what we have done is, with bipartisan efforts, is work together and, again, not caring who gets the credit for what, as we accomplish things up there.

And that's been just a part of the operation that I wanted to participate in. And that's what we're going to do in Washington, D.C., also, bring in both sides together. John McCain is known for doing that, also, in order to get the work done for the American people.

IFILL: Let's come full circle. You both want to bring both sides together. You both talk about bipartisanship. Once again, we saw what happened this week in Washington. How do you change the tone, as vice president, as number-two?

BIDEN: Well, again, I believe John McCain, were he here— and this is a dangerous thing to say in the middle of an election—but he would acknowledge what I'm about to say.

I have been able to work across the aisle on some of the most controversial issues and change my party's mind, as well as Republicans', because I learned a lesson from Mike Mansfield.

Mike Mansfield, a former leader of the Senate, said to me one day—he—I made a criticism of Jesse Helms. He said, "What would you do if I told you Jesse Helms and Dot Helms had adopted a child who had braces and was in real need?" I said, "I'd feel like a jerk."

He said, "Joe, understand one thing. Everyone's sent here for a reason, because there's something in them that their folks like. Don't question their motive."

I have never since that moment in my first year questioned the motive of another member of the Congress or Senate with whom I've disagreed. I've questioned their judgment.

I think that's why I have the respect I have and have been able to work as well as I've been able to have worked in the United States Senate. That's the fundamental change Barack Obama and I will be bring to this party, not questioning other people's motives.

IFILL: Governor?

PALIN: You do what I did as governor, and you appoint people regardless of party affiliation, Democrats, independents, Republicans. You—you walk the walk; you don't just talk the talk.

And even in my own family, it's a very diverse family. And we have folks of all political persuasion in there, also, so I've grown up just knowing that, you know, at the end of the day, as long as we're all working together for the greater good, it's going to be OK.

But the policies and the proposals have got to speak for themselves, also. And, again, voters on November 4th are going to have that choice to either support a ticket that supports policies that create jobs.

You do that by lowering taxes on American workers and on our businesses. And you build up infrastructure, and you rein in government spending, and you make our—our nation energy independent.

Or you support a ticket that supports policies that will kill jobs by increasing taxes. And that's what the track record shows, is a desire to increase taxes, increase spending, a trillion-dollar spending proposal that's on the table. That's going to hurt our country, and saying no to energy independence. Clear choices on November 4th.

IFILL: Governor Palin, you get the chance to make the first closing statement.

PALIN: Well, again, Gwen, I do want to thank you and the commission. This is such an honor for me.

And I appreciate, too, Senator Biden, getting to meet you, finally, also, and getting to debate with you. And I would like more opportunity for this.

I like being able to answer these tough questions without the filter, even, of the mainstream media kind of telling viewers what they've just heard. I'd rather be able to just speak to the American people like we just did.

And it's so important that the American people know of the choices that they have on November 4th.

I want to assure you that John McCain and I, we're going to fight for America. We're going to fight for the middle-class, average, everyday American family like mine.

I've been there. I know what the hurts are. I know what the challenges are. And, thank God, I know what the joys are, too, of living in America. We are so blessed. And I've always been proud to be an American. And so has John McCain.

We have to fight for our freedoms, also, economic and our national security freedoms.

It was Ronald Reagan who said that freedom is always just one generation away from extinction. We don't pass it to our children in the bloodstream; we have to fight for it and protect it, and then hand it to them so that they shall do the same, or we're going to find ourselves spending our sunset years telling our children and our children's children about a time in America, back in the day, when men and women were free.

We will fight for it, and there is only one man in this race who has really ever fought for you, and that's Senator John McCain.

IFILL: Thank you, Governor. Senator Biden.

BIDEN: Gwen, thank you for doing this, and the commission, and Governor, it really was a pleasure getting to meet you.

Look, folks, this is the most important election you've ever voted in your entire life. No one can deny that the last eight years, we've been dug into a very deep hole here at home with regard to our economy, and abroad in terms of our credibility. And there's a need for fundamental change in our economic philosophy, as well as our foreign policy.

And Barack Obama and I don't measure progress toward that change based on whether or not we cut more regulations and how well CEOs are doing, or giving another $4 billion in tax breaks to the Exxon Mobils of the world.

We measure progress in America based on whether or not someone can pay their mortgage, whether or not they can send their kid to college, whether or not they're able to, when they send their child, like we have abroad—or I'm about to, abroad—and John has as well, I might add—to fight, that they are the best equipped and they have everything they need. And when they come home, they're guaranteed that they have the best health care and the best education possible.

You know, in the neighborhood I grew up in, it was all about dignity and respect. A neighborhood like most of you grew up in. And in that neighborhood, it was filled with women and men, mothers and fathers who taught their children if they believed in themselves, if they were honest, if they worked hard, if they loved their country, they could accomplish anything. We believed it, and we did.

That's why Barack Obama and I are running, to re-establish that certitude in our neighborhoods.

Ladies and gentlemen, my dad used to have an expression. He'd say, "champ, when you get knocked down, get up."

Well, it's time for America to get up together. America's ready, you're ready, I'm ready, and Barack Obama is ready to be the next president of the United States of America.

May God bless all of you, and most of all, for both of us, selfishly, may God protect our troops.

IFILL: That ends tonight's debate. We want to thank the folks here at Washington University in St. Louis, and the Commission on Presidential Debates.

There are two more debates to come. Next Tuesday, October 7th, with Tom Brokaw at Belmont University in Nashville, and on October 15th at Hofstra University in New York, with Bob Schieffer.

Thank you, Governor Palin and Senator Biden. Good night, everybody.

Alaska Governor Resignation Speech

July 3, 2009

Hi Alaska, I appreciate speaking directly to you, the people I serve, as your Governor.

People who know me know that besides faith and family, nothing's more important to me than our beloved Alaska. Serving her people is the greatest honor I could imagine.

I want Alaskans to grasp what can be in store for our state. We were purchased as a territory because a member of President Abe Lincoln's cabinet, William Seward, providentially saw in this great land, vast riches, beauty, strategic placement on the globe, and opportunity. He boldly looked "North to the Future". But he endured such ridicule and mocking for his vision for Alaska, remember the adversaries scoffed, calling this "Seward's Folly". Seward withstood such disdain as he chose the uncomfortable, unconventional, but right path to secure Alaska, so Alaska could help secure the United States.

People who know me know that besides faith and family, nothing's more important to me than our beloved Alaska.

Alaska's mission—to contribute to America. We're strategic in the world as the air crossroads of the world, as a gatekeeper of the continent. Bold visionaries knew this—Alaska would be part of America's great destiny.

Our destiny to be reached by responsibly developing our natural resources. This land, blessed with clean air, water, wildlife, minerals, AND oil and gas. It's energy! God gave us energy.

So to serve the state is a humbling responsibility, because I know in my soul that Alaska is of such import, for America's security, in our very volatile world. And you know me by now, I promised even four years ago to show my independence... no more conventional "politics as usual".

And we are doing well! My administration's accomplishments speak for themselves. We work tirelessly for Alaskans.

We aggressively and responsibly develop our resources because they were created to be used to better our world... to help people... and we protect the environment and Alaskans foremost with our policies.

Here's some of the things we've done:

We created a petroleum integrity office to oversee safe development. We held the line for Alaskans on Point Thomson—and finally for the first time in decades—they're drilling for oil and gas.

We have AGIA, the gas line project—a massive bi-partisan victory—also succeeding as intended—protecting Alaskans as our clean natural gas will flow to energize us, and America, through a competitive, pro-private sector project. This is the largest private sector energy project, ever. This is energy independence.

And ACES—another bipartisan effort—is working as intended and industry is publicly acknowledging its success. Our new oil and gas "clear and equitable formula" is so Alaskans will no longer be taken advantage of. ACES incentivizes new exploration and development and jobs that were previously not going to happen with a monopolized North Slope oil basin.

We cleaned up previously accepted unethical actions; we ushered in bi-partisan Ethics Reform.

We also slowed the rate of government growth, we worked with the Legislature to save billions of dollars for the future, and I made no lobbyist friends with my hundreds of millions of dollars in budget vetoes... but living beyond our means today is irresponsible for tomorrow.

We took government out of the dairy business and put it back into private-sector hands—where it should be.

We provided unprecedented support for education initiatives, and with the right leadership, finally filled long-vacant public safety positions. We built a sub-Cabinet on Climate Change and took heat from Outside special interests for our biologically-sound wildlife management for abundance.

We broke ground on the new prison.

And we made common sense conservative choices to eliminate personal luxuries like the jet, the chef, the junkets... the entourage.

And the Lt. Governor and I said "no" to our pay raises. So much success in this first term—and with this success I am proud to take credit... for hiring the right people! Our goal was to achieve a gas line project, more fair oil and gas valuation, and ethics reform in four years. We did it in two. It's because of the people... good public servants surrounding the Governor's office, with servants' hearts and astounding work ethic... they are Alaska's success!

We are doing well! I wish you'd hear more from the media of your state's progress and how we tackle Outside interests— daily—special interests that would stymie our state. Even those debt-ridden stimulus dollars that would force the heavy hand of federal government into our communities with an "all-knowing attitude"—I have taken the slings and arrows with that unpopular move to veto because I know being right is better than being popular. Some of those dollars would harm Alaska and harm America—I resisted those dollars because of the obscene national debt we're forcing our children to pay, because of today's Big Government spending; it's immoral and doesn't even make economic sense!

Another accomplishment—our Law Department protected states' rights—two huge U.S. Supreme Court reversals came down against that liberal Ninth Circuit, deciding in our state's favor over the last two weeks. We're protectors of our Constitution—federalists protect states' rights as mandated in 10th amendment.

But you don't hear much of the good stuff in the press anymore, do you?

Some say things changed for me on August 29th last year— the day John McCain tapped me to be his running-mate—I say others changed.

Let me speak to that for a minute.

Political operatives descended on Alaska last August, digging for dirt. The ethics law I championed became their weapon of choice. Over the past nine months I've been accused of all sorts of frivolous ethics violations—such as holding a fish in a photograph, wearing a jacket with a logo on it, and answering reporters' questions.

Every one—all 15 of the ethics complaints have been dismissed. We've won! But it hasn't been cheap, the State has wasted thousands of hours of your time and shelled out some two million of your dollars to respond to "opposition research", that's money not going to fund teachers or troopers—or safer roads. And this political absurdity, the "politics of personal destruction" ... Todd and I are looking at more than half a million dollars in legal bills in order to set the record straight. And what about the people who offer up these silly accusations? It doesn't cost them a dime so they're not going to stop draining public resources—spending other peoples' money in their game.

It's pretty insane—my staff and I spend most of our day dealing with this instead of progressing our state now. I know I promised no more "politics as usual," but this isn't what anyone had in mind for Alaska.

If I have learned one thing: life is about choices!

And one chooses how to react to circumstances. You can choose to engage in things that tear down, or build up. I choose to work very hard on a path for fruitfulness and productivity. I choose not to tear down and waste precious time; but to build UP this state and our country, and her industrious, generous, patriotic, free people!

Life is too short to compromise time and resources... it may be tempting and more comfortable to just keep your head down, plod along, and appease those who demand: "Sit down and shut up", but that's the worthless, easy path; that's a quitter's way out. And a problem in our country today is apathy. It would be apathetic to just hunker down and "go with the flow".

Nah, only dead fish "go with the flow".

No. Productive, fulfilled people determine where to put their efforts, choosing to wisely utilize precious time... to build up.

And there is such a need to build up and fight for our state and our country. I choose to fight for it! And I'll work hard for others who still believe in free enterprise and smaller government; strong national security for our country and support for our troops; energy independence; and for those who will protect freedom and equality and life... I'll work for and campaign for those proud to be American, and those who are inspired by our ideals and won't deride them.

I will support others who seek to serve, in or out of office, for the right reasons, and I don't care what party they're in or no party at all. Inside Alaska—or outside Alaska.

But I won't do it from the Governor's desk.

I've never believed that I, nor anyone else, needs a title to do this—to make a difference... to help people. So I choose, for my State and my family, more "freedom" to progress, all the way around... so that Alaska may progress... I will not seek re-election as Governor.

And so as I thought about this announcement that I wouldn't run for re-election and what it means for Alaska, I thought about how much fun some governors have as lame ducks... travel around the state, to the Lower 48, overseas on international trade—as so many politicians do. And then I thought—that's what's wrong—many just accept that lame duck status, hit the road, draw the paycheck, and "milk it". I'm not putting Alaska through that—I promised efficiencies and effectiveness! ? That's not how I am wired. I am not wired to operate under the same old "politics as usual." I promised that four years ago—and I meant it.

It's not what is best for Alaska.

I am determined to take the right path for Alaska even though it is unconventional and not so comfortable.

With this announcement that I am not seeking re-election... I've determined it's best to transfer the authority of governor to Lieutenant Governor Parnell; and I am willing to do so, so that this administration—with its positive agenda, its accomplishments, and its successful road to an incredible future—can continue without interruption and with great administrative and legislative success.

My choice is to take a stand and effect change—not hit our heads against the wall and watch valuable state time and money, millions of your dollars, go down the drain in this new environment. Rather, we know we can effect positive change outside government at this moment in time, on another scale, and actually make a difference for our priorities—and so we will, for Alaskans and for Americans.

Let me go back to a comfortable analogy for me—sports... basketball. I use it because you're naïve if you don't see the national full-court press picking away right now: A good point guard drives through a full court press, protecting the ball, keeping her eye on the basket... and she knows exactly when to pass the ball so that the team can win. And I'm doing that—keeping our eye on the ball that represents sound priorities—smaller government, energy independence, national security, freedom! And I know when it's time to pass the ball—for victory.

I have given my reasons candidly and truthfully... and my last day won't be for another few weeks so the transition will be very smooth. In fact, we will look to swear Sean in—in Fairbanks at the conclusion of our Governor's picnics.

I do not want to disappoint anyone with my decision; all I can ask is that you trust me with this decision—but it's no more "politics as usual".

Some Alaskans don't mind wasting public dollars and state time. I do. I cannot stand here as your Governor and allow millions upon millions of our dollars go to waste just so I can hold the title of Governor. And my children won't allow it either. ? Some will question the timing. ? Let's just say, this decision has been in the works for awhile...

In fact, this decision comes after much consideration, and finally polling the most important people in my life—my children . It was four "yes's" and one "hell yeah!" The "hell yeah" sealed it—and someday I'll talk about the details of that... I think much of it had to do with the kids seeing their baby brother Trig mocked by some pretty mean-spirited adults recently. Um, by the way, sure wish folks could ever, ever understand that we all could learn so much from someone like Trig—I know he needs me, but I need him even more... what a child can offer to set priorities right—that time is precious... the world needs more "Trigs", not fewer.

My decision was also fortified during this most recent trip to Kosovo and Landstuhl, to visit our wounded soldiers overseas, those who sacrifice themselves in war for our freedom and security... we can all learn from our selfless Troops... they're bold, they don't give up, they take a stand and know that life is short so they choose to not waste time. They choose to be productive and to serve something greater than self... and to build up their families, their states, our country. These Troops and their important missions—those are truly the worthy causes in this world and should be the public priority with time and resources and not this local / superficial wasteful political bloodsport.

May we ALL learn from them!

First things first: as Governor, I love my job and I love Alaska. It hurts to make this choice but I am doing what's best for Alaska. I've explained why... though I think of the saying on my parents' refrigerator that says "Don't explain: your friends don't need it and your enemies won't believe you anyway."

But I have given my reasons... no more "politics as usual" and I am taking my fight for what's right—for Alaska—in a new direction.

Now, despite this, I don't want any Alaskan dissuaded from entering politics after seeing this real "climate change" that began in August... no, we need hardworking, average Americans fighting for what's right! And I will support you because we need you and you can effect change, and I can too on the outside.

We need those who will respect our Constitution where government's supposed to serve from the bottom up, not move toward this top down big government take-over... but rather, will be protectors of individual rights—who also have enough common sense to acknowledge when conditions have drastically changed and are willing to call an audible and pass the ball when it's time so the team can win! And that is what I'm doing!

Remember Alaska... America is now, more than ever, looking North to the Future. It'll be good. So God bless you, and from me and my family—to all Alaska—you have my heart.

And we will be in the capable hands of our Lieutenant Governor, Sean Parnell. And Lieutenant General Craig Campbell will assume the role of Lieutenant Governor. And it is my promise to you that I will always be standing by, ready to assist. We have a good, positive agenda for Alaska.

In the words of General MacArthur said, "We are not retreating. We are advancing in another direction."

Tea Party Convention Keynote

February 6, 2010

I am so proud to be an American! Thank you so much for being here tonight!

Do you love your freedom?!

If you love your freedom, think of that.

Any of you here serving in uniform, past or present, raise your hand. We're going to thank you for our freedom. God bless you guys! We salute you! We honor you. Thank you.

I am so proud to be American. Thank you. Gosh, thank you.

Happy birthday, Ronald Reagan!

Well, a special hello to the C-SPAN viewers. You may not be welcome in those health care negotiations, but you have an invitation to the Tea Party.

Very good to be here in Tennessee, the volunteer state. It's the home of good country music and good southern barbecue and—great to be at the Tea Party Convention. I guess down here that's some southern sweet tea. And you know up in Alaska, we have a smaller version of Tea Party up there. We call it "iced tea." And I am a big supporter of this movement. I believe in this movement. Got lots of friends and family in the lower 48 who attend these events and across the country just knowing that this is the movement and America is ready for another revolution—and you are a part of this.

I look forward to attending more Tea Party events in the near future. It is just so inspiring to see real people—not politicos, not inside-the-Beltway professionals—come out and stand up and speak out for common-sense conservative principles.

And today, I want to start off with a special shout-out to American's newest Senator, thanks to you, Scott Brown. Now in many ways Scott Brown represents what this beautiful movement is all about. You know, he was just a guy with a truck and a passion to serve our country. He looked around and he saw that things weren't quite right in Washington. So, he stood up and he decided that he was going to do his part to put our government back on the side of the people. And it took guts. And it took a lot of hard work. But with grassroots support, Scott Brown carried the day.

And it has been so interesting now to watch the aftermath of the Massachusetts Chowder Revolution. The White House blames the candidate —their candidate. And Nancy Pelosi, she blamed the Senate Democrats. And Rahm Emanuel, he criticized a pollster. And yet again, President Obama found some way to make this all about George Bush. You know, considering the recent conservative election sweep, it's time that they stop blaming everyone else. When you're 0-for-3, you'd better stop lecturing and start listening.

The only place that the Left hasn't placed the blame is on their agenda. So, some advice for our friends on that side of the aisle: That's where you got to look because that's what got you into this mess—the Obama-Pelosi-Reid agenda. It's going to leave us less secure, more in debt, and more under the thumb of big government. And that is out of touch, and it's out of date. And if Scott Brown is any indication, it's running out of time.

Because from Virginia to New Jersey to Massachusetts, voters are sending a message up and down the East Coast and in good places like Nevada and Connecticut and Colorado, Michigan, North Dakota, they've got the Liberal Left—that establishment—running scared. The bottom line is this: It's been a year now. They own this now and voters are going to hold them accountable. Because out here in the cities and in the towns across this great country, we know that we've got some big problems to solve. We've gotten tired now of—of looking backward. We want to look forward. And from here, my friends, the—the future—it looks really good. It looks really good because if there's hope in Massachusetts, there's hope everywhere.

Brown's victory—it's exciting, and it's a sign of more good things to come. A lot of great common sense conservative candidates, they're going to put it all on the line in 2010. This year, there are going to be some tough primaries. And I think that's good. Competition in these primaries is good. Competition makes us work harder and be more efficient and produce more. And I hope you'll get out there and work hard for the candidates who reflect your values, your priorities—because despite what the pundits want you to think, contested primaries aren't civil war. They're democracy at work, and that's beautiful.

I was the product of a competitive primary where, running for governor, I faced five guys in the party, and we put our ideas and our experience out there on the table for a debate, and then we allowed, of course, the voters to decide. And that is a healthy process, and it gives Americans the kind of leadership that they want and deserve. And so in 2010, I tip my hat to anyone with the courage to throw theirs in the ring, and may the best ideas and candidates win.

But while I hope that you're going to give these candidates that you choose your best effort, please understand that they're human. There's no perfect candidate, and they're going to disappoint occasionally. And when they do, let them know, but don't get discouraged and sit it out, because the stakes are too high. The stakes are too high right now, and your voice is too important. So work hard for these candidates, but put your faith in ideas.

And in that spirit, I caution against allowing this movement to be defined by any one leader or politician. The Tea Party movement is not a top-down operation. It's a ground-up call to action that is forcing both parties to change the way that they're doing business, and that's beautiful. This is about the people. This is about the people, and it's bigger than any king or queen of a Tea Party. And it's a lot bigger than any charismatic guy with a teleprompter.

The soul of this movement is the people—everyday Americans who grow our food and run our small businesses, teach our kids, and fight our wars. They're folks in small towns and cities across this great nation who saw what was happening—and they saw and were concerned, and they got involved. Like you, they go to town hall meetings, and they write op-eds. They run for local office. You all have the courage to stand up and speak out. You have a vision for the future, one that values conservative principles and common sense solutions. And if that sounds like you, then you probably too are feeling a bit discouraged by what you see in Washington D.C.

Now in recent weeks, many of us have grown even more uneasy about our Administration's approach to national security, the most important role ascribed to our federal government. Let me say, too, it's not politicizing our security to discuss our concerns, because Americans deserve to know the truth about the threats that we face and what the Administration is or isn't doing about them. So let's talk about them.

New terms used like "overseas contingency operation" instead of the word "war." That reflects a worldview that is out of touch with the enemy that we face. We can't spin our way out of this threat. It's one thing to call a pay raise a job created or saved. It's quite another to call the devastation that a homicide bomber can inflict a "manmade disaster." And I just say, come on, Washington. If nowhere else, national security—that's one place where you got to call it like it is.

And in that we spirit—in that spirit we should acknowledge that on Christmas Day, the system did not work. Abdul Mutallab passed through airport security with a bomb, and he boarded a flight hell-bent on killing innocent passengers. This terrorist trained in Yemen with Al Qaida, his American visa was not revoked until after he tried to kill hundreds of passengers. On Christmas Day, the only thing that stopped this terrorist was blind luck and brave passengers. Really, it was a Christmas miracle, and that is not the way that the system is supposed to work.

What followed was equally disturbing. After he was captured, he was questioned for only 50 minutes. We had a choice in how to do this. The choice was, only question him for 50 minutes and then read his Miranda Rights. The Administration says then, there are no downsides or upsides to treating terrorists like civilian criminal defendants.

But a lot of us would beg to differ. For example, there are questions we would have liked this foreign terrorist to answer before he lawyered up and invoked our U.S. Constitutional right to remain silent. *Our* U.S. Constitutional rights. Our rights that you, sir [to male veteran in audience] fought and were willing to die for to protect in our Constitution. The rights that my son, as an infantryman in the United States Army is willing to die for. The protections provided —thanks to you, sir—we're going to bestow them on a terrorist who hates our Constitution and tries to destroy our Constitution and our country? This makes no sense because we have a choice in how we're going to deal with the terrorists. We don't have to go down that road.

There are questions that we would have like answered before he lawyered up like: "Where exactly were you trained and by whom? You—You're bragging about all these other terrorists just like you. Who are they? When and where will they try to strike next? The events surrounding the Christmas Day plot reflect the kind of thinking that led to September 11th. That...the...threat then, as the USS Cole was attacked, our Embassies were attacked, it was treated like an international crime spree, not like an act of war. We're seeing that mindset again settle into Washington. That scares me for my children and for your children. Treating this like a mere law enforcement matter places our country at grave risk. Because that's not how radical Islamic extremists are looking at this. They know we're at war. And to win that war, we need a Commander-in-Chief, not a professor of law standing at the lectern.

It's that same kind of misguided thinking that is seen throughout the Administration's foreign policy decisions. Our President spent a year reaching out to hostile regimes, writing personal letters to dangerous dictators, and apologizing for America. And what do we have to show for that? Here's what we have to show. North Korea tested nuclear weapons and longer range ballistic missiles. Israel, a friend and a critical ally, now question[s] the strength of our supports. Plans for a missile defense system in Europe? They've been scrapped. Relations with China and Russia are no better. And relations with Japan—that key Asian ally— they're in the worse shape in years.

And around the world, people who are seeking freedom from oppressive regimes, wonder if Alaska is still that beacon of hope for their cause. The Administration cut support for democracy programs, and where the President has not been clear, I ask, where is his clear and where is his strong voice of support for the Iranians who are risking all in their opposition to Ahmadinejad?

Just that short list—that short list. And you know, it's no wonder that our President only spent about nine percent of his State of the Union Address discussing national security and foreign policy, because there aren't a whole lot of victories that he could talk about that night. And that's just a short list.

There are so many challenges in front of us, and it can seem overwhelming. But despite these challenges, we have hope that we can move things in the right direction. But it's going to require the Administration to change course. We need a foreign policy that distinguishes America's friends from her enemies and recognizes the true nature of the threats that we face.

We need a strong national defense. I think you would agree with me, as—as Reagan used to talk about that "peace through strength." And in that respect, I applaud the President for following at least a part of the recommendations made by our commanders on the ground to send in some more reinforcements to Afghanistan. Now, though he, we must spend less time courting our adversaries, spending more more time working with our allies. And we must build effective coalitions capable of confronting dangerous regimes like Iran and North Korea. It's time for more than just tough talk. Just like you—probably just so tired of hearing the talk, talk, talk. Tired of hearing the talk.

It's time for some tough actions, like sanctions on Iran. And in places in the world where people are struggling and oppressed and they're fighting for freedom, America must stand with them. We need a clear foreign policy that stands with the people and for democracy—one that reflects both our values and our interests, and it is in our best interests, because democracies—they don't go to war with each other. They can settle their differences peacefully.

The lesson of the last year is this: Foreign policy can't be managed through the politics of personality. And our President would do well to take note of an observation John F. Kennedy had made once he was in office: that all the world's problems aren't his predecessor's fault. The problems that we face in the real world require real solutions. And we'd better get to it, because the risks that they pose are great and they're grave. However, as Barry Goldwater said: "We can be conquered by bombs...but we can also be conquered by neglect by ignoring our constitution and disregarding the principles of limited government."

And in the past year, his words rang true. Washington has now replaced private irresponsibility with public irresponsibility. The list of companies and industries that the government is crowding out and bailing out and taking over, it continues to grow. First it was the banks, mortgage companies, financial institutions, then automakers. Soon, if they had their way, health care, student loans.

Today, in the words of Congressman Paul Ryan, The 700 billion dollar "TARP has morphed into crony capitalism at its worse." And it's becoming a "slush fund" for the Treasury Department's favorite big players, just as we had been warned about. And while people on Main Street look for jobs, people on Wall Street—they're collecting billions and billions in your bailout bonuses. Among the top 17 companies that received your bailout money, 92 percent of the senior officers and directors—they still have their good jobs.

And everyday Americans are wondering: Where are the consequences? They helped to get us into this worst economic situation since the Great Depression. Where are the consequences?

When Washington passed a 787 billion dollar "stimulus bill," we were nervous because they just spent 700 billion dollars to bailout Wall Street. And on the state level, as a governor, we knew that a lot of that money came with fat strings attached. The federal government was going to have more control over our states. They were going to disrespect the 10th Amendment of our Constitution by essentially bribing us with, "Take this federal money" (and then we're going to be able to mandate a few more things on you though.)

I joined with other conservative governors around the nation in rejecting some of those dollars. Legislators—Turned out to be, though, nothing for applause because—nothing to applaud because—legislators then were threatening lawsuits if governors didn't take the money. And I vetoed some of the funds that—I knew we couldn't maintain the programs, that we were going to pay for it with these—these borrowed, printed up, invented dollars out of nowhere. But lawsuits were threat—even in Alaska, in a Republican controlled legislature, my veto was overridden and the money poured into those states. And I believe we will see this play out in our states: The federal government will have taken more control over the people who live in our states.

Now I understand wanting to believe that this is all free money. And for some I guess it's tough to tell people no in tough times. Plus, remember our Administration promised that it would be good stewards of tax payer dollars. Remember? Remember Vice President Biden. He was put in charge of a tough, unprecedented oversight effort. That's how it was introduced. You know why? Because nobody messes with Joe.

Now, this was all part of that hope and change and transparency. And now a year later I've got to ask those supporters of all that: How's that hopey-changey stuff working out for you? See, I tried to look into that transparency thing, but Joe's meetings with the transparency and accountability board—it was closed to the public. Yeah, they held the transparency meeting behind closed doors. So, not sure if anybody's messing with Joe, but here is what I do know: A lot of that stimulus cash—it ended up in some pretty odd places, including districts that didn't even exist; and programs that really don't have a whole lot to do with stimulating the economy.

Nearly six million dollars was given to a democrat pollster who had already made millions during the Democrats' presidential primary. Nearly 10 million was spent to update the stimulus web site. And one state even spent a million bucks to put up signs that advertised that they were spending the federal stimulus projects. Or as someone put it: This was a million dollar effort using your money to tell you it's spending your money. And it didn't create a single job.

These uses of stimulus funds don't sound targeted and they don't sound timely, as we were promised. They just sound wasteful. And in the case of those signs, kind of ridiculous. All of that—I don't know about you, but seeing seeing those checks written for some of these pet projects of congressmen and those in the White House—did you feel very stimulated?

And then it turns out that Washington got the price tag wrong. All of these projects and programs, they cost tens and tens of billions of dollars more than we were told. It's now closer to 860 billion dollars. Add this to the fact that the White House can't even tell us how many jobs were actually created. Depending on who you ask, it's anywhere from thousands to two million.

But one number we are sure of is the unemployment number. And that's at 9.7, which is well above the 8 percent mark that we were promised our stimulus package would go to avoid. And unemployment now is—underemployment now is 16.5 percent. You've got all these people who have just kind of given up right now, and they're not even enrolling in some of these programs. Tough to count them.

Folks, I won't go into all of it tonight, but the list of broken promises is long. Candidate Obama pledged to end closed-door, sweetheart deals and no-bid contracts once and for all, But just last month his Administration awarded a 25 million dollar no-bid contract to a Democrat donor. Is that hope? Nope. It's not hope.

That's the same old, same old in Washington, D.C. And instead of changing the way Washington does business, we got the "Cornhusker Kickback" and the "Louisiana Purchase" and millions of tax breaks for union bosses' desires. The promised ban on lobbyists in this new Administration, he handed out waivers left and right, and there are more than 40 former lobbyists who now work at the top levels in this Administration. And these days most members of Congress, they don't get to read the bill before they have to vote on it, much less the pledge that a bill wouldn't be signed into law until we all had five days to review it online.

So see, it's easy to understand why Americans are shaking their heads when Washington has broken trust with the people that these politicians are to be serving. We're drowning in national debt and many of us have had enough.

Now the foundational principles in all of this, it's easy to understand. It really is—even I though I think D.C. would just love for us to believe that this is all way over our heads. Somebody in Tennessee, somebody up there in Alaska, she'll never understand what we're talking about here in D.C. No, this is all pretty simple stuff. When our families, when our small businesses, we start running our finances into the red, what do we do? We tighten our belts and we cut back budgets. Isn't that what we teach our children—to live within our means? It's what Todd and I do when we have to make payroll, buy new equipment for our commercial fishing business. We have to plan for the future, meet a budget.

But in Washington, why is it just the opposite of that? This week, they unveiled a record-busting, mindboggling 3.8 trillion dollar federal budget. And they keep borrowing, and they keep printing these dollars, and they keep making us more and more beholden to foreign countries, and they keep making us take these steps towards insolvency. Now what they're doing in proposing these big new programs with giant price tags, they're sticking our kids with the bill. And that's immoral. That's generational theft. We're stealing the opportunities from our children.

And freedom lovers around this country need to be aware that all of this makes us more beholden to other countries. It makes us less secure. It makes us less free. And that should tick us off. So folks, with all these serious challenges ahead, we've got private-sector job creation that has got to take place and got these economic woes and—and health care, the war on terror.

But as the saying goes, if you can't ride two horses at once, you shouldn't be in the circus. So here's some advice for those in D.C. who want to shine in the greatest show on earth. Too often when big government and big business get together and cronyism sets in, well, it benefits insiders, not everyday Americans. The Administration and Congress should do what we did up there in Alaska when the good old boys started making back room deals that were benefiting big oil and not the citizens of the state. And the citizens of the state then, Alaskans, we got together and we put government back on the side of the people. And a lot of the big wigs, they started getting in trouble and some of the big wigs ended up going to jail over their back room deals.

Our government needs to adopt a pro-market agenda that doesn't pick winners and losers, but it invites competition and it levels the playing field for everyone. Washington has got to across the board, lower taxes for small businesses so that our mom and pops can reinvest and hire people so that our businesses can thrive. They should support competition, support innovation, reward hard work.

And they should do all that they can to make sure that the game is fair without that undo corrupt influence. And then they need to get government out of the way. If they would do this—If they would do this, our economy, it would roar back to life and for instance on health care, we need bipartisan solutions to help families, not increase taxes. Remember that red reset button that America through Secretary Clinton, she gave to Putin. Remember that? I think we should ask for that back and hand it instead to Congress. And say, no, start all over on this health care scheme and pass meaningful, market-based reforms that incorporate some simple steps that have broad support, the—the best ideas, not back room deals but things like insurance purchases across state lines and the tort reform that we've talked about.

Those things that are common sense steps towards reform that the White House and—and leaders on—on the Democrats' side of—of the aisle in Congress, they don't want to consider. So it makes you wonder, what truly is their motivation? What is their intention if they won't consider even these common sense, broad-based support ideas that would work? And to create jobs. Washington should jump start energy projects. I said it during the campaign and I'll say it now: We need an "all of the above" approach to energy policy. That means proven conventional resource development and support for nuclear power. And I was thankful that the President at least mentioned nuclear power in the State of the Union.

But, again, we need more than words. We need a plan to turn that goal into a reality and that way we can pave the way for projects that will create jobs. Those are real job creators and deliver carbon free energy. And while we're at it, let's expedite the regulatory and permitting and legal processes for on and offshore drilling. Instead of paying billions of dollars, hundreds of billions of dollars that now are being sent to foreign regimes, we should be drilling here and drilling now instead of relying on them to develop their resources for us. So what we've got to do is axe that plan for cap-and-tax, that policy that's going to kill jobs and is going to pass the burden of paying for it onto our working families.

And finally, if we're going to get serious about fiscal restraint, then we've got to make Washington start walking the walk. After putting us on a track to quadruple the deficit, the proposed spending freeze, maybe it's a start, but it's certainly not enough. As Senator John Thune said, it's like putting a Band-Aid on a self- inflicted gunshot wound.

We need to go further. Cut spending. Don't just simply slow down a spending spree. And we've got to axe the plans for a second stimulus when the first hasn't even been measured for any success yet. Kill the plans for the second stimulus and be aware that now that second stimulus is being referred to as a "jobs bill." Now these aren't the only ways to rein in spending, and alone, they're not going to be enough, not enough to tackle the insane debt and the deficits that we face. But they are a good way to start and to show that we're serious about getting our financial house in order.

Now like a lot of you, perhaps, I have spent the last year thinking about how—how to best serve. How—How can I help our country? How can I make sure that I, that you, that we're in a position of nobody being able to succeed? When they try to tell us to sit down and shut up, how can we best serve? In 2008, I had the honor—really of a lifetime—the honor of a lifetime, running alongside John McCain. I...look at him as an American hero. And nearly 60 million Americans voted for us. They cast their ballot for the things that we are talking about tonight: lower taxes, smaller government, transparency, energy independence and strong national security.

And while our votes did not carry the day, it was still a call to serve our country. Those voters wanted us to keep on fighting and take the gloves off. They wanted common sense conservative solutions. And they wanted us to keep on debating. And each of us who is here today, we're living proof that you don't need an office or a title to make a difference. You don't need a proclaimed leader, as if we're just a bunch of sheep looking for a leader to progress this movement.

That is what we're fighting for. It is what we are fighting about. It is what we believe in and that's what this movement is all about. When people are willing and to meet halfway and stand up for common sense solutions and values, then we want to work with them. And in that spirit, I applaud Independents and Democrats like Bark Stupak who stood up to tough partisan pressure and he wanted to protect the sanctity of life and the rights of the soon to be born. I applaud him for that.

When we can work together, we will. But when the work of Washington violates our—our conscience and when the work and efforts in Washington, D.C., violate our Constitution, then we will stand up and we will be counted—because we are the loyal opposition. And we have a vision for the future of our country, too, and it is a vision anchored in time tested-truths: that the government that governs least, governs best. And that the Constitution—the Constitution provides the best road map towards a more perfect union. And that only a limited government can expand prosperity and opportunity for all. And that freedom is a God-given right and it is worth fighting for. God bless you. And that America's finest, our men and women in uniform, are a force for good throughout the world—and that is nothing to apologize for.

These are enduring truths and these enduring truths have been passed down from Washington to Lincoln to Reagan and now to you. But while this movement, our roots there, in our spirit, too, they are historic. The current form of this movement is fresh and it's young and it's fragile. We are now the keepers of an honorable tradition of conservative values and good works. And we must never forget that it is a sacred trust to carry these ideas forward. It demands civility and it requires decent, constructive, issue-oriented debate.

Opponents of this message, they're seeking to marginalize this movement. They want to paint us as ideologically extreme and the counterpoint to liberal intolerance and outrageous conspiracy theorists aimed at our own government and unethical shameless tactics like considering a candidate's children fair game.

But unlike the elitists who denounce this movement—they just don't want to hear the message—I've traveled across this great country and I've talked to the patriotic men and women who make up the Tea Party movement. And they are good and kind and selfless and they are deeply concerned about our country. And today I ask only this: Let's make this movement a tribute to their good example and make it worthy of their hard work and their support.

Do not let us have our heads turned from the important work before us and do not give others an excuse to be able to turn their eyes from this. Let us not get bogged down in the small squabbles. Let us get caught up in the big ideas.

To do so would be a fitting tribute to Ronald Reagan, especially tonight, as he would have turned 99. No longer with us, his spirit lives on and his American dream endures. He knew the best of our country is not all gathered in Washington, D.C. It is here in our communities where families live, and children learn, and children with special needs are welcomed in this world and embraced. And thank you for that.

The best of America can be found in places where patriots are brave enough and free enough to be able to stand up and speak up; and where small businesses grow our economy one job at a time; and folks like Reagan, we know that America is still that "shining city on a hill." I do believe that God "shed his grace on thee." We know that our best days are yet to come. Tea Party nation, we know that there is nothing wrong with America that together we can't fix as Americans.

So from the bottom of my heart and speaking on behalf of millions and millions and millions of Americans who want to encourage this movement, this movement is about the people. Who can argue a movement that is about the people and for the people? Remember, all political power is inherent in the people, and government is supposed to be working for the people. That is what this movement is about.

From the bottom of my heart, I thank you for being part of the solution. God bless you, Tea Partiers and God bless the USA.

Thank you. God bless you guys.

Charity of Hope: Ontario Canada

Friday, April 16, 2010

I don't know if I should Buenos Aires or Bonjour, or... this is such a melting pot. This is so beautiful. I love this diversity. Yeah. There were a whole bunch of guys named Tony in the photo line, I know that. And in the introduction too, in the instructions to you all, I got a kick out of the instruction "No heckling." I am so used to the heckling, it's okay! We're used to it. They just hit you into the boards and maybe get called for a penalty or whatever, but we can handle that too.

But this reminds me of heading out on stage on the VP trail when I was getting ready to debate Joe Biden. And there were like 40 some million viewers that I knew were out there waiting to see "is she going to crash? Is she going to be able to handle herself? How's it going to go?" Whenever we go and do something big in life, like a vice presidential debate—it's kind of big—I like to say a prayer about it, you know. I need some divine inspiration and I need to remember what it really is all about, so that evening before the debate I remember being back stage and looking around for somebody to pray with. And looking around at the campaign staff and there's nobody to prayer with.

But backstage there was Piper, at the time my seven year old. And I told Piper, I tried to make it easy for her to understand, I said "Piper, kay, I'm going out on stage. I'm debatin' this guy, it's going to be kind of tough." I said, "So pray with me, honey." And I grabbed her hands because that's what we always do, we pray together. I said "Piper, just pray that I win." Cause you know, why not?! Just pray that I do well, and oh man, try and keep it easy, I said "Just pray that God just speaks right through me." And Piper said "God, speaking through you? That would be cheating."

Not that I would ever think that God would speak through me, but wanting to leave you with a little bit of inspiration and encouragement and maybe on a personal level have a conversation with you about some of the things that Todd and I have been through in the last year and a half, the last couple of years, that hopefully you can learn a couple of lessons from, because we've been through quite a few challenges, quite a few battles and you all too, everybody goes through battles, everybody has challenges. Some are played out in the newspapers, some of ours have been. Maybe yours have not been.

But everybody has to make tough decisions and prioritize things in life and here we are tonight, given an opportunity to come together to reach out to help others, to help children, who are in need. We don't want to squander this opportunity, we want to be inspired and encourage and remember that though we all do go through some tough challenging times, we talked at the head table tonight that we need to be able to count our blessings, not our problems.

It's gorgeous here and you can just feel the hospitable spirit that is part of this town and I know that you are known for volunteerism and to help one another. Looking out at the landscape, I became so impressed you know with God's country, this is gorgeous, and already having met some great people, thinking how lucky you all are. But I'm also looking out my hotel window and I'm overlooking Copps Colliseum and I'm thinking, What a great place for an NHL franchise! You're all set up for it. I'd come in for the first face off, we'd love to be a part of it, so you know if ever I run into the president of the NHL, yeah, I'll put a little bug in his ear, okay. We'll do that.

My favorite quote, coach Lou Holtz from Notre Dame, and I know there are a couple of guys here who love Notre Dame, yeah. Well Coach Holtz, he had said that God did not put us on this earth to be ordinary, he expects great things from us. He's not going to drive parked cars, either. We shouldn't just sit around in a parked car and have him do something for us.

No, you need opportunities to get out there and be productive and to contribute and he expects us not to be boring and depressed and not productive. He didn't put us on this earth to be ordinary. And you, being here tonight, an example of those who are extraordinary because you're part of an event tonight that is extraordinary. It's an opportunity to reach out and help children, and I don't think there is anything more important in life than helping children. So meeting Carmen's team and you all helping with this charity, it's inspiring to me.

Very, very good though, to be in Canada, our Alaskan neighbor. I know that maybe others in the U.S. love Canada too, but who loves Canada more than your neighbor there in Alaska? We have such a great connection with you all, I think we share so much. With wildlife and resources and again with that work ethic and that pioneering spirit that just flows through Canada, that's my state too, that's Alaska. That's the way we live and we're brought up. And um, our accents too. You know how many people ask me on the campaign trail if I was Canadian? They think that we talk alike. We say 'eh' too, in Alaska. Never thought anything of it until some reporters.

But too, my first five years of life were spent right there on the border of Canada, right next to you all, but further away. My dad was a school teacher so he went up there to teach school so we spent time on that connection between the two countries and we would travel East often, so many times drive the Alaska-Canada highway, loving that beautiful road trip and when I got older, participating in the Klondike road race.

Relatives from Canada, too. We have the foundation of the Palin family, one grandfather was born in Manitoba, this was a farming family there. And then another one born in Saskatchewan and we were some pretty funny stories of our relatives who were bootleggers I guess. This was many, many years ago. Don't blame me. There's never a boring story when it comes to the Palins.

But I want to tell you, on behalf of the United States, how much we appreciate you. One thing, thank you for hosting our American athletes and athletes from all over the place in the wonderful Olympics that you did such a good job. Thank you so much. It was a beautiful event and it gave the world the opportunity to find out what Alaskans already knew that Canada is the beautiful place. It's special and it's a wonderful place and it's full of some tough and talented hockey players, too. And congratulations on taking gold in hockey. [applause] It was palm worthy [holds up hand to reveal writing]. I had to remind myself on that one: Be nice about the Olympic gold. I promised that I would.

Both our countries love that tough tenacious sport. And Todd and I spent some good hockey time with kids here over the years. It's healthy competition. Yeah, you beat us from time to time on the ice, but coming in second team USA I thought they had nothing to apologize for.

In about one year's time span, what Todd and I have gone through...You think, wow, there could be some lessons could be learned in this. First of all I was very, very busy. I was governor of Alaska and not having been elected at a relatively young age, at the time looking back I think I was young back then when I was first elected, it seems eons ago. Being governor of the largest state to the Union and Todd was really busy.

For many years Todd has worked up on the oil fields in Prudo Bay, up on the north slope of Alaska. Many weeks up on the north slope. In fact it's the equivalent of about six months on the north slope and then six months home, but when he's home his job is a commercial fisherman in Bristol Bay, another tough, blue collar, hard core job. So he's very busy with his vocations and allocations, in addition to being Alaska's First Dude.

Todd is so cool because one of the tea parties he attended he had just come off the airplane and had tea at the White House with the first ladies including Mrs. Bush. He had just gotten off the snowmobile race, he's the four time world champion of snow-machine racing, the longest snow-machine race in the world, it's 2,000 miles across Alaska. Very rugged. He had broken his arm with 400 miles to go in the race and had finished the race and then got it casted.

So he ripped his cast off before the tea party with Mrs. Bush and it was just cracking me up thinking, man, if only people knew, the way that we really live. But he's pretty amazing that he's been able to multitask like that. In fact, his commute from the governor's mansion was about 1,700 miles. That's how big Alaska is and that's how long his commute was so that added to it.

Well, while I was younger I was busy, I was the chairman of the state's oil and gas commission, so dealing on a national level with oil and gas issues. Having four kids, our oldest son, Track, who grew up obsessed with hockey. He too, like all of us hockey moms, he just thought he was going to be the next Wayne Gretzky. And don't we all think our kids going to be that and we don't want to take that dream away from them because life can suck a dream out of a kid, a mom, a dad, we shouldn't be the one to diminish that dream, so encouraging him, travelling all over the nation and he doing really well. He just turned 18 and finally his last shoulder surgery, his injury had just, it, it, reality set in.

So, he decides on September 11 that he's going to enlist in the United States army as an infantry man. He's barely 18 years old and that just kind of rocked my world. And it all of a sudden, shifted in me that perspective on what was going on in the world and how important peace is and we don't want to send our sons and our daughters to war unless there is a good purpose to this. So Track enlisted in the army and he was to deploy to Iraq in a year, in a war zone, the next September 11. And it filled in me such an appreciation for country, for patriotism, such an appreciation for understanding freedom isn't free, and we do have to fight for our freedom and there is great sacrifice involved in that. That's what his enlistment and then his deployment, he being gone for a year in a war zone, taught me...

I found out that I was pregnant. And here I was no spring chicken, you know? So, that was kind of another earth-shattering experience to go through, all in one year. And I'm

111

thinking "dang it" I didn't know what to think, it was surreal. But I'm thinking I'm 43 years old, I know what the critics are going to say, they're going to say "there Alaska goes, they finally elect the first woman governor and she goes and gets herself pregnant." I knew the criticism would come but I knew I could handle that. Five kids, right on, the more the merrier. Todd and I love kids. Gosh, we just live for children and for helping children.

Well, about 12 weeks along in the pregnancy, Todd was in Canada, a vo-tech school in Edmonton. I went to the doctor and he said well we've got some test results for you and you need to sit down and just be prepared. And I thought, I've never been sick a day in my life, everything's going to be fine. And she told me the baby's going to be born with Down syndrome. So that's another thing that just sort of, wow, shattered my world for a minute, because I was scared to death. I said "wait a minute God, I didn't order this." How in the world am I going to handle this? Never in my wildest dreams would I have thought we would be in that situation.

And my sister has a child with autism and one of my thought's was, "God, my sister is the one who is compassionate and she has more time and she's kind of wired to deal with a child with special needs. I don't think I am. And unless you change my heart, God, I don't think I'm going to be able to handle this one." But having to hold onto faith that I had always talked about and preached about and thought I believed in, that God wouldn't give us something we couldn't handle. For Todd, when he returned from Canada, I said Todd, aren't you thinking 'Why us?" And he said "Why not us?" And that shifted perspective right off the bat too, again thinking we are privileged and we are blessed.

I didn't tell anybody I was pregnant until I was seven months along and I knew people thought I was getting chubby but they were too nice to say anything. There we are in February, March, in Alaska and I'm just wearing more layers. They're just thinking I'm cold all the time and I'm pregnant seven months. And then Trig came five weeks early so people thought I was only pregnant for like three weeks. And to this day some people still don't think that the baby is my own, believe it or not.

He's got this heart of gold. Here is the lesson that I learned from Trig, besides being more compassionate and really wanting to reach out and help those who have challenges and maybe are less privileged or have less ability than others. Oh my gosh. But this is the lesson we all can learn from Trig and I do know that he'll be teaching us more than we're ever going to be able to teach him. One thing he teaches us, he wakes up in the morning, he kind of looks around and rubs his sleepy little eyes, and he starts applauding. And I think "Oh my goodness, we should all have that perspective." So I watch this little boy and I learn so much from him: he applauds the day! He's just a blast, he's so much fun.

So that all happened in one year's time. And in that year, just a few weeks after Trig was born, my teenage daughter, my perfect teenage daughter, great athlete, great student, hard working girl, just in case you never read it in the tabloids, I'll break the news to ya: My teenage daughter comes to us, to Todd and me, and she says, "what's the worst thing you can think of?" And of course, lots of bad things popped into my mind. She was smart to say it that way, because by the time she told us she was pregnant it was like, oh, okay.

The governor's daughter tells us she's pregnant and that rocked our world, because you're selfishly thinking "no, you're not the one who's supposed to be pregnant, maybe one of your friends, but not you Bristol." Wow, when it rains it pours. What are you preparing us for? What are you trying to teach us? I think what he was whispering in my ear was "are you going to walk the walk, or are you just going to talk the talk?"

Now she's got the most beautiful little baby and I still can't believe I'm a grandma! And I'm kind of glad Tripp doesn't talk yet because I'm not sure what he's going to call me. But it's teaching me to be less judgmental. She knows she did something she wishes she wouldn't have done for ten years from now, because these are less than ideal circumstances. It's very tough on a teenage mom who's trying to make it on her own. A huge percentage of teenage girls do not have the resources that Bristol has, but she's taken responsibility and a lot of other people take responsibility. It's less than ideal but you make the right choice and then it does work out.

But all of these "life happens" events all in one year. I'm thinking, I don't know what's around the next corner, but nothing can be bigger than what we just went through. And then I get the call from John McCain and he asks if I want to run for vice president of the United States of America. Just another little thing that happens in a year.

Every day of that campaign I learned more and more about purpose and handling situations that seem less than ideal, but having to have faith that nothing is an accident and that everything that happens in our lives is to put us on a path that we were created to do, and we never know the outcome, no idea, no guarantees, no promises of where things will end up. But what an interesting year that he had, certainly teaching me too, as Plato had said: Be nice to everyone, because everyone has a challenge, a battle...But just know that everyone has a situation where there's something going on in their life where they could use a touch, they could use a positive, a reaffirming word and action to let them know that you care.

Some of the days we've had over the last year or two, we've had to just say to each other, Man, just hold on because morning is coming and we have to believe that there is a brighter day ahead. And we're living that out. There have been very bright days. Getting to be here today. Somebody asked me tonight, How do you take the mocking and the political potshots and the kind of constant criticism? And I said, because look where I am today! I'm in Hamilton with the most wonderful people, with their heart in the right place, wanting to help others. I'll take all that other stuff because I know we're on the right path.

Some of these media saying things about me, I know what the truth is. And I will take that, if that's kind of the price that has to be paid to be in a position where I can help others. So again, just being so extremely grateful for the situations we have gone through, though at the time, seeming less than ideal not knowing if I would ever get to a point of being really grateful. We certainly are grateful now.

In seriousness, too, I want to talk about what I've learned as an American, and what I see as a relationship building opportunity that we have between America and Canada, because I think as nations we're getting closer together. We all will be given even more opportunities to help those who are in need, who have less privilege than many of us have. I'm very grateful for the strong bond between our two countries. Ronald Regan once remarked that Canada and the United States share more than a common border, we share a democratic tradition and hopes and dreams and aspirations of a free people. And he said that hope has made a difference in our lives.

That's why we're here tonight. And remember that bond of hope and that love of freedom between our countries has withstood the test of time. Today we're proud to work with you culturally and economically as partners, and as a trading partner and security ally in NATO. I want to tell you that we're thankful to have our young men and women in uniform too, serving alongside your young men and women, your sons and daughters. I don't know if you hear it enough from the US, how much we appreciate you, your sons, your daughters, who are fighting terrorists, who want to bring peace on earth, and it is peace through strength that's needed right now, but the sacrifices made by the country of Canada, as so many of your families making such sacrifice to allow this service in the war on terror.

Especially your 142 warriors who have paid the ultimate sacrifice who have come from Canada, our hearts go out to those families and words cannot suffice, but we appreciate this. Certainly as a mom of a son having recently returned from his year-long deployment in Iraq too, with the army, I thank you for your efforts and for our relationship there. I know that that one isn't easy, again with words not being able to suffice. Except to say thank you.

But our country really does appreciate our neighbor. In the lower 48 states, they say to the north. In Alaska, we say just right next door. We appreciate our neighbors. A recent poll had asked Americans, which country do you like best? Other than America. Where would you go? And 90 per cent picked Canada. [applause] We do have so much in common. We both love good hunting and fishing and that great outdoors. And we love the amazing creation that is the north. The true north strong and free, as you all say. And we respect too, the talent and creativity of Canadians.

I get a kick out of telling. First, our unusual cultures really have benefited from the contributions and the arts and the sports coming from Canada. In fact, recently, I was in one of Canada's most populous cities: which is Los Angeles, believe it or not. LA, population wise, is one of your top 15 most Canadian populated areas in the whole world. And you send us your celebrities and your screen writers, and your film makers, and every four years our celebrities start saying 'come election time, I'm moving to Canada if the election results don't come out the way that I want them." You can imagine there were many celebrities saying that the last time around with John McCain and I were running. But they didn't have to move, their team won.

But for Alaska and Canada having so much in common, and having worked together on some of the most important infrastructure projects in the world. And one of those is the Al-Can highway. Every time my kids and my Todd, we've driven the Alaska-Canada highway, which is our link to the rest of the world really, it reminds my kids that highway isn't just a road, it really is a lifeline. And it was one of the most ambitious projects ever. Certainly the most ambitious project taken at the time of World War II, in terms of infrastructure. The Al-Can highway went from just a thought on paper to, within 26 days, being able to start ramming through that road.

In less than a year, with 10,000 American troops and Canadian troops and civilians they carved a road out of the wilderness that has been a lifeline. They worked seven days a week, around the clock, in frigid temperatures, with swarms of mosquitoes. It was perseverance, it was that work ethic

117

back then. And when it was done, we finally had a key piece of infrastructure that helped secure and defend the North American continent, really, certainly Alaska.

The highway represents that special kinship between our countries and today that bond continues with another enormous project that's going on right now, and that's an Alaskan gas line. And Alaska and Canada both understand the importance of developing both of our area's energy resources responsibly and safely, to keep our part of the world safe and secure and free so that we're not relying on dangerous foreign sources of energy. And that's why, after I served on the Wasilla city council, then I served as a mayor, a city manager, and then an oil and gas state commissioner, and then finally as the elected governor of Alaska.

One of the pillars of my platform all the way through that was to ramp up production, to ramp up industry with our energy resources. And that included getting that pipeline underway, to finally get it off the diving board. It had talked about it for fifty years. Getting it off so it can finally bring an energy resource to hungry markets, and there are trillions of cubic feet of natural gas line in tact in these areas that will be developed, and geologists saying that there are hundreds of trillions more undiscovered both on shore and off shore. Just piles of energy in that part of North America that again can be tapped responsibly and make us all secure and make us more prosperous and make us more free.

So we opened up the process while I was the governor with great transparency. And this is on the heels of eliminating a lot of corruption in our state government. It all had to do with oil and gas. A lot of the big wigs in Alaska's political circles and some business community members they ended up going to jail because of those being purchased and just some untoward actions with oil and gas development and we cleaned up corruption and I think I'm a busy mom as governor, I just didn't have time for all the things that were on the periphery that maybe some politicians want to get involved in. No, I just wanted to get the job done. No time for the drama in all the power plays, just get from point A to point B, get the job done and clean up the corruption.

Through this transparent process, we wanted to get out there on the world market and essentially have the world, who would be the best pipe line builder in the world to tap resources and allow them to flow into hungry markets? And through this process, an exclusive basis went to TransCanada was chosen, out of everybody in the world, it was TransCanada!

There's still lots of work to be done, but it's going to help production, it's going to help industry and it will provide all of us a better, healthier way of life and it is still in the works. We would not have come this far after 50 years of hoping for it, had it not been for Canadian ingenuity and that work ethic that proved in a competitive process that this company, from Calgary, had known what was best to tap resources. So I thank you for that. It is a mutually beneficial project.

The project is just one example of what we can do in terms of economic recovery. And America must really start concentrating on economic recovery and creating jobs because there are major economic woes in our country right now and certainly that adversely affects Canada too. It is time to re-tap our abundant domestic resources and send them to hungry markets at home and share competitively in the marketplace with our friends and allies. And doing so will make us less beholden to dangerous foreign regimes that could cut off energy supply at any time that they wanted.

It's amazing to consider what's here in Canada too, untapped, and your tar sands, and the richness, the vastness, that you have in terms of amounts of energy that can still be tapped. There's more energy here than really there is in Saudi Arabia when you consider what's in the tar sands. And you guys have great potential here. You have the skill. You have great workers. You have everything in place to ramp up development and allow more job creation and allowance. Energy is so important.

I know Canadians understand this, but there is an inherent link between energy and prosperity and energy and security, and energy and freedom. And development isn't the only part of the equation. As governor I had to advocate the three point approach to meeting energy needs with conservation and responsible resource development and promotion of renewable energy sources. But as we do this together, it will give us more opportunity for a better life, a healthier life, a more prosperous life. And then we can voluntarily share that better life with others who are in need. Tonight being a picture of opportunity to share with others.

One of the things I've been able to do is attend these Tea Parties across the US events. It's just been invigorating and energizing and some of them are just a hoot. Some of the signs we read out there in the rallies. One of them I saw yesterday said "I can see freedom from my house." I think they were quoting Tina Fey on that one. The other one said "the voters are coming, the voters are coming." And that was exclusive to Boston. The hecklers are funnier than heck too. Usually if there's a bad poster out there I pretend I don't even see it. But yesterday I could not miss it. They were these life-size pictures of naked people. I was like, okay, that one is effective—I can't... they caught me off guard on that one.

Other than that, and the stuff that goes on on the periphery. These Tea Parties have been an amazing manifestation of America's pioneering spirit, where we're saying we don't want government to make us work for them, we want our government to work for us, we want them back on our side.

The Tea Party are an important gathering of Americans who are really part of this grassroots people's movement, it's a conservative movement, but those involved in it, are parties, from independents. Like Todd's not even registered in the party and people tell me I am the worst recruiter of the Republican Party if I can't even get my own husband to join.

But more power to him. He's an independent. But this movement that's sweeping the nation, getting to be a part of that is really awesome. I wanted to talk to and here from those whom natural resources and freedom and work ethic are so important. And what's going on in our country we can't wait even another day just being complacent and think that everything's just going to magically work out for us, because they won't. We're spending too much money, we've got too much debt and we've got to start ramping up industry and reigning in the spending.

In our cities and in our towns, citizens understand this and they're standing up and they're speaking out on behalf of commonsense conservative solutions. Not really difficult things. Ronald Regan had said, there are no easy answers but there are simple answers. We just need the courage to do what we know is morally right.

Relying on major foreign regimes to meet our energy needs makes no sense, because it makes all of us less secure. And it costs us hundreds and hundreds of billions of dollars every year asking the Saudis or Chavez to ramp up production so that we can purchase from them. We say no more. When it comes to something this important, we have to give it our all. And that's a focus of mine as I go forward. And then we look at Canada, and we being so impressed with how you too have embraced the renewables, the alternatives, you've investing in real science and real projects that can be reliable and economic to keep our environment clean, to reduce emissions. The US can look at what Canada is doing and take a strong steps forward in this arena.

There are areas where we disagree, no doubt, and when disagreements arise thankfully we get to talk openly as allies, as friends, as neighbors, we can talk about these things openly as good friends do. And we're always looking out for one another, seeking ways to help one another and seeking common ground. The heart of the friendship is created really an unbreakable bond between us. And I think former US president John F. Kennedy, he put it best, when he had said, "American and Canada, geography made us neighbors, history has made us friends, economics has made us partners and necessity has made us allies."

I do believe that if he was here to look down us on today and see us here in Hamilton, I think he's pleased to see that bond of friendship, it endures, and it can manifest itself in opportunity to provide for others in need. Now then, we can each do our part and set up to preserve what we have already started for the rest generation.

We North Americans we come from the stock of our ancestors. My husband, he's Alaskan native. He's Eskimo. And then my Idaho roots. And I look out here and man, this melting pot and I recognize all our diverse backgrounds. And North America and our countries together, it's playing a role in history of all of us, and we share the ideals of freedom and prosperity and sharing with others. It's great places like Hamilton that make up the fabric of our nations. So knowing that there are many challenges in the years to come, through strength and perseverance, we're going to continue to hold the global stage and our responsibility to stand up for what's right.

This is our charge. This is our responsibility. This is part of our destiny and it's why we're all here tonight. It's not coincidental. There's purpose. We've been given a responsibility by our forefathers to carry the torch, to protect our core principals. We have to hold that torch in each of our own hearts, of generosity and kindness and helping children and never letting anyone tell you to sit down and shut up and tell you that you can't do it.

Restoring Honor Rally

August 28, 2010

Thank you so much. Are you not so proud to be an American?

What an honor. What an honor.
We stand today at the symbolic crossroads of our nation's history. All around us are monuments to those who have sustained us in word or deed. There in the distance stands the monument to the father of our country. And behind me, the towering presence of the Great Emancipator who secured our union at the moment of its most perilous time and freed those whose captivity was our greatest shame. And over these grounds where we are so honored to stand today, we feel the spirit of Dr. Martin Luther King, Jr., who on this very day, two score and seven years ago, gave voice to a dream that would challenge us to honor the sacred charters of our liberty—that all men are created equal.

Now, in honoring these giants, who were linked by a solid rock foundation of faith in the one true God of justice, we must not forget the ordinary men and women on whose shoulders they stood. The ordinary called for extraordinary bravery. I am speaking, of course, of America's finest—our men and women in uniform, a force for good in this country, and that is nothing to apologize for.

Abraham Lincoln once spoke of the "The mystic chords of memory, stretching from every battle-field, and patriot grave, to every living heart and hearthstone, all over this broad land." For over 200 years, those mystic chords have bound us in gratitude to those who are willingly to sacrifice, to restrain evil, to protect God-given liberty, to sacrifice all in defense of our country.

They fought for its freedom at Bunker Hill, they fought for its survival at Gettysburg, and for the ideals on which it stands—liberty and justice for all—on a thousand battlefields far from home.

It is so humbling to get to be here with you today, patriots—you who are motivated and engaged and concerned, knowing to never retreat. I must assume that you too know that we must not fundamentally transform America as some would want. We must restore America and restore her honor!

Now, I've been asked to speak today, not as a politician. No, as something more—something much more. I've been asked to speak as the mother of a soldier, and I am proud of that distinction. You know, say what you want to say about me, but I raised a combat vet, and you can't take that away from me. I'm proud of that distinction, but it is not one that I had imagined because no woman gives birth thinking that she will hand over her child to her country, but that's what mothers have done from ancient days.

In cities and towns across our country, you'll find monuments to brave Americans wearing the uniforms of wars from long ago, and look down at their inscriptions, you'll see that they were so often dedicated by mothers. In distant lands across the globe, you'll find silent fields of white markers with the names of Americans who never came home, but who showed their dedication to their country by where they died.

We honor those who served something greater than self and made the ultimate sacrifice, as well as those who served and did come home forever changed by the battlefield. Though this rally is about "restoring honor," for these men and women honor was never lost! If you look for the virtues that have sustained our country, you will find them in those who wear the uniform, who take the oath, who pay the price for our freedom.

And I'd like to tell you three stories of such Americans—three patriots—who stand with us today.

The first is a man named Marcus Luttrell. His story is one of raw courage in the face of overwhelming odds. It's also a story of America's enduring quest for justice. Remember, we went to Afghanistan seeking justice for those who were killed without mercy by evil men on September 11th. And one fateful day in Afghanistan on a mountain ridge, Marcus and three of his fellow Navy SEALs confronted the issue of justice and mercy in a decision that would forever change their lives.

They were on a mission to hunt down a high-level Taliban leader, but they were faced with a terrible dilemma when some men herding goats stumbled upon their position, and they couldn't tell if these men were friend or foe. So the question was what to do with them? Should they kill them or should they let them go and perhaps risk compromising their mission? They took a vote. They chose mercy over self-preservation. They set their prisoners free. The vote said it was the humane thing to do. It was the American thing to do. But it sealed their fate because within hours, over a hundred Taliban forces arrived on the scene. They battled the four Navy SEALs throughout the surrounding hills. A rescue helicopter came, but it was shot down. By the time the sun set on June 28, 2005, it was one of the bloodiest days for American forces in Afghanistan.

19 brave, honorable men were lost that day. Marcus was the sole survivor. Alone, stranded, badly wounded, he limped and crawled for miles along that mountain side. What happened next is a testament to the words: "Blessed are the merciful, for they shall be shown mercy." Marcus and his team showed mercy in letting their prisoners free. And later he was shown mercy by Afghan villagers who honored an ancient custom of providing hospitality to any stranger who would ask for it. They took him in. They cared for him, refused to hand him over to the Taliban. They got him back safely to our forces.

Marcus' story teaches us that even on the worst battlefield against the most brutal enemy, we adhere to our principles. This American love of justice and mercy is what makes us a force for good in this world. Marcus is a testament to that.

Please join me in honoring retired U.S. Navy SEAL Petty Officer Marcus Luttrell.

From the time he first heard men marching to a cadence call, Eddie Wright had one dream in life, and that was to be a United States Marine. And as a Marine serving in Iraq, his company was ambushed in Fallujah. He was knocked out when a rocket propelled grenade hit his Humvee. When he came to, he saw that both his hands were gone and his leg was badly wounded.

He couldn't fire his weapon, he could barely move, and he was bleeding to death. But he had the strength of mind to lead the men under his command, and that is exactly what he did. He kept them calm, he showed them how to stop the bleeding in his leg, he told them where to return fire, he had them call for support, and he got them out of there alive.

His composure under fire that day earned him the Bronze Star with Valor device. But if you ask him, "What did you get it for?" he'll tell you, "Just for doing my job."

After a long recovery, Eddie continued to serve as a martial arts instructor. He resigned from his beloved Marine Corps a few years ago, but he still lives by the motto: "Once a Marine, always a Marine."

And if you want to see the American spirit of never retreating, no matter the odds—of steady confidence and optimism, no matter the setbacks—look at Eddie's story. No matter how tough times are, Americans always pull through. As Eddie put it himself: "We don't really foster the attitude of I can't. When you have an obstacle in front of you, you just keep putting one foot in front of the other, and focus on what you can."

So, please join me in honoring retired Marine Sergeant James "Eddie" Wright.

Tom Kirk was an Air Force squadron commander and a combat pilot who had flown over 150 missions in Korea and Vietnam. One day on a routine mission over Hanoi, his plane was shot down. He spent the next five and a half years in that living hell known as the Hanoi Hilton.

Like his fellow prisoners, Tom endured the beatings, the torture, the hunger, the years of isolation. He described it, saying, "There was nothing to do, nothing to read, nothing to write. You had to just sit there in absolute boredom, loneliness, frustration, and fear. You had to live one day at a time, because you had no idea how long you were going to be there."

After two years of solitary confinement, pacing back and forth in his cell—three and a half steps across, three and a half steps deep—Tom was finally moved to a larger holding cell with 45 other Americans prisoners, among them was a man named John McCain. In circumstances that defy description, this band of brothers kept each other alive, and one by one, they came home.

Tom was released on March 14, 1973. You might think that a man who had suffered so much for his country would be bitter and broken by it. But Tom's heart was only filled with love—love for America—that special love of country that we call patriotism.

Tom wrote, "Patriotism has become, for many, a 'corny' thing. For me, it is more important now than at any time in my life. How wonderful it is to be an American come home!"

Friends, please join me in honoring retired Air Force Colonel Tom Kirk.

My fellow Americans, each one of these men here today faced terrible sufferings, overwhelming set-backs, and impossible odds.

And they endured! And their stories are America's story.

We will always come through. We will never give up, and we shall endure because we live by that moral strength that we call grace. Because though we've often skirted a precipice, a providential hand has always guided us to a better future.

And I know that many of us today, we are worried about what we face. Sometimes our challenges, they just seem insurmountable.

But, here, together, at the crossroads of our history, may this day be the change point!

Look around you. You're not alone. You are Americans!

You have the same steel spine and the moral courage of Washington and Lincoln and Martin Luther King. It is in you. It will sustain you as it sustained them.

So with pride in the red, white, and blue; with gratitude to our men and women in uniform; let's stand together! Let's stand with honor! Let's restore America!

God bless you! And God bless America!

Printed in Great Britain
by Amazon